JOY
—LIKE A—
MOUNTAIN

Unleash the Power of Biblical Joy on the Journey of Life

TALASI GUERRA

KIROS PUBLISHING

ISBN: 978-1-7772059-0-4 (paperback)
ISBN: 978-1-7772059-2-8 (hardcover)
ISBN: 978-1-7772059-3-5 (ebook)

Cover Design by 100Covers.com
Interior Design by FormattedBooks.com

Do you need a quick boost of biblical joy?

JOIN THE 7-DAY JOY CHALLENGE TODAY!

Sign up for **FREE** at:
https://www.talasiguerra.com/7dayjoychallenge

For Avra.
May you always find joy
on the mountain of life.

CONTENTS

Chapter 1: The Genesis 1
Chapter 2: The Goal 15
Chapter 3: The Guarantee 29
Chapter 4: The Guide 45
Chapter 5: The Gear 59
Chapter 6: The Guts 75
Chapter 7: The Grit 91
Chapter 8: The Glory 107

Conclusion 123
Acknowledgements 127
Endnotes 129

The Genesis

J oy has never come naturally to me.

When I was a child, back in the days of chalkboards and cage-free trampolines, I remember singing a Sunday school song that went like this:

> "I've got peace like a river,
> I've got love like an ocean,
> I've got joy like a fountain in my soul."

It was a great song with some fun actions, but the truth is that these lyrics presented a conundrum for me because it was impossible to sing them honestly. Peace like a river, love like an ocean, and joy like a fountain in my soul? Even if I ignored the first two claims, both of which seemed equally out of reach, the third statement could have tipped me over the edge of personal guilt.

I didn't have joy like a fountain. I didn't even have joy like a leaky faucet or a dollar store squirt gun. In fact, for many years of my life, joy seemed like a lost cause.

It began as an attack on my self-worth when I was just a child. Like that time in third grade when my small-town Sunday school class prepared a song for the Christmas concert at church and each of us was chosen to dress up as one of the animals from the manger scene. I couldn't have been happier with my assignment! Of all the messy, stinky, embarrassing barnyard animals I might have been, I was handpicked to play the soft and delicate dove.

Then one day at school, a boy from my Sunday school class told the other kids about our upcoming production. Beaming with pride and dignity, I chimed in to announce my role as the esteemed dove. But to my great horror, that boy looked at me in front of our classmates and said with the kind of insensitivity that only an eight-year-old boy could muster up, "Oh, I thought you were going to be the donkey!"

Now, this might seem like an inconsequential childhood memory, but I've never forgotten that moment. I cried about it in my bed that night, with my mom at my side trying to reassure me that I still had value and worth. But in that moment, I believed I was nothing but a donkey. A big, ugly, stupid donkey.

I wish I could say that I learned, through this childhood experience or others like it, that it really didn't matter what other people thought of me. I wish I had learned in that moment that joy was a choice, regardless of my circumstances. But unfortunately, that didn't happen. I just got older. And the "donkey" moments became more frequent, but less juvenile. They became heavier and more damaging.

Instead of a little boy calling me a donkey, the media started calling me fat and ugly. Perfectionism informed me that I could never measure up. Boys began to communicate that my worth came from my appearance and the accessibility of my body. My guilt enlightened me to the fact that, since I had made a few bad choices, I was no longer worthy of God's love.

Joy evaded me through elementary and middle school. Constantly plagued by one heartache or another, I started to wonder if things would ever get better. Then, what might have started out as your average adolescent angsty behavior, quickly took a turn for the worse when I developed an eating disorder by the age of fourteen. And if there's one thing I know about living with binge-purge type anorexia, it's that you're not exactly the life of the party.

In fact, in my case, I wanted nothing to do with parties at that stage. Parties meant people, food, and awkward clothes that showed off the body I hated. But all I wanted to do was hide away in my room with a bowl of popcorn and a bottle of diet Sprite until I could sneak into the bathroom unnoticed and ever-so-quietly flush the memory of that disgusting binge down the toilet, only to punish myself for it later.

This destructive cycle continued into adulthood, and by the time I was twenty-one, I had hit rock bottom. Parties were a different thing now—a place to drown my sorrows and seek the attention I so desperately craved. My life was an unqualified mess, laden with addictions, anxiety, and depression. Even after I finally recovered from my eating disorder in 2007 and managed to get my physical health back on track, I still had a long way to go when it came to internal healing.

Needless to say, joy was a challenge.

JOY LIKE A ~~FOUNTAIN~~ MOUNTAIN

The idea that I could experience life-giving, unbridled joy was never even a possibility in my mind. Joy was nothing like a fountain that welled up within me and poured out to the world around me.

If anything, I saw joy more like an enormous mountain that people like me, try as we might, would never be able to climb. The spectacular view from the summit was scarcely more than a figment of my imagination because only a lucky few would ever make it there. And I wasn't one of those people. So, I wondered, *Why bother with the first few steps of the journey if I know I'm not cut out for the climb?*

Maybe at some point in your life you've asked yourself that same question. Maybe, like me, you've had a difficult relationship with the concept of joy, and you're just not convinced that it's worth the effort anymore. Maybe you've read everything the Bible has to say about joy, but, for some reason, you just can't seem to apply it to your life in a meaningful way that sticks. And maybe, ever so slowly, you've begun to lose hope in the idea of joy altogether, surrendering to the lie that real joy is out of reach for someone like yourself.

If any of that sounds familiar, this book is for you.

This book is for the brave souls who are willing to examine the current level of joy in their lives and admit that it comes up short. This book is for parents who can see the effects of their own joylessness taking root in the hearts of their children but feel utterly helpless to stop it. This book is for anyone who relates to the idea that discovering joy is much more like an arduous climb up a steep, unforgiving mountain than a refreshing dip in a clean, sparkling fountain.

This book is for you because this book is for me. What I mean is that, in a sense, I am you… or, at least, I have been. I've been in all of those places. I've felt hopelessness sink in as I succumbed to the lie that true, biblical joy would never be possible for me.

But I was wrong. And I've never been happier to admit it!

After years of living under this oppressive mindset, God began to challenge my thinking. Exposing the lies that controlled my mind and showing me where my life didn't line up with his word, he began asking me to explore the pursuit of intentional, biblical joy.

So that's what I did. After numerous prods and nudges, I developed an intensive personal joy challenge to immerse myself in for an entire month. It was life-changing! Not only did I quickly begin to experience more joy, but I also made tons of powerful discoveries that have altered the trajectory of my life forever.

One of the things I learned is that, as it turns out, I was partly right about the fact that I'm not cut out to climb the impossible mountain of joy. In fact, none of us are, really, but not in the way I thought at first.

The reason none of us are cut out to scale this mysterious mountain is because it doesn't actually exist. Yes, the experience of discovering joy does often feel like climbing a mountain. It can be difficult and laborious, and, sometimes, it can even feel downright impossible. But when we think of joy as the mountain itself, we miss the whole point of the analogy: Joy is not a destination to arrive at but a means by which we can complete a journey.

Joy is *like* a mountain. But the idea that we must reach the summit to achieve mountaintop joy is a myth fed to us by the devil himself to distract us from what's really going on down here. See, we're all on a mountain; that part is true. But the mountain is not joy. The mountain is simply life.

THE MOUNTAIN OF LIFE

We're all on a journey up the mountain of life.

The idea is that one day we'll reach the peak of our lives (the top of the mountain) and be able to look back on the journey with a sense of satisfaction and gratitude for what we've accomplished. But sadly, too many people don't make it that far. Buckling under the weight of their baggage or immobilized by fear at the sight of a rocky cliff or a perilous pass, they simply give up along the way.

I've seen far too many people stop right where they are, in the middle of the mountain, and admit defeat, sometimes moments before a breakthrough. Instead of reaching out for the help and tools they need to conquer the obstacle they face, they concede. "It's over. I've come as far as I'll go. I give up."

These people tend to live lives of regret. They go through the rest of their days wondering what might have happened if they had kept going. Instead of experiencing the fulfillment and satisfaction of reaching the summit, they settle for a comfortable plateau and lose sight of their purpose.

The truth is that we all have moments on the mountain when we want to give up. We all experience highs and lows, ups and downs, wins and losses. Most of us find ourselves living on a plateau at least for a season. But we don't have to stay there. We don't have to concede. Because it's not over, and we're still on the mountain. At any moment, we can pick up where we left off and face the giants we fear.

But how do we do that? When the going gets tough, when the storm clouds brew, when the mountain hits us with an avalanche of adversity, how can we hold it together and press on? How can we pick up the pieces, push through the pain, and prevail over the mountain rather than peter out at a plateau?

That's what this book is all about. In the pages that follow, I'm going to share with you what I believe is one of the key secrets to conquering the mountain of life.

Now, you might be thinking, *Wait a minute. I thought I picked up a book about joy. What does joy have to do with all of this?*

Friend, my answer is simple:

Everything.

Over and over, throughout the Bible, God prescribes joy for his people. As our creator, he knows that joy is in our best interest. He understands the disastrous effects that neglecting joy can have on our physical, mental, and spiritual health.

Proverbs 17:22 says, "A joyful heart is good medicine, but a crushed spirit dries up the bones" *(ESV)*. And this isn't just a nice Bible verse; it's scientifically proven! Research shows that joy actually makes you healthier! Aside from the positive effects joy has on your brain, circulatory system, and autonomic nervous system,[1] studies also show that happier people are more likely to live a healthy lifestyle, have stronger immune systems, and do a better job of dealing with stress.[2]

It's no wonder that God has so much to say about joy in his word! He's the architect who drew up the blueprints for how joy would affect our bodies, minds, and spirits. When God commands us to be joyful (Phil. 4:4) or to not be anxious (Phil. 4:6), he does so for our own good because he knows that without joy, our bones will dry up, which is really just a poetic way of saying that we'll start to waste away internally and eventually die.

DEAD MEN WALKING

Without joy, we're like dead men walking. When we let the hardships and obstacles that we face on the mountain drain us of life, rather than seeing them as an opportunity to take a dose of the "good medicine" that Proverbs 17:22 prescribes, we effectively sign our own death certificates.

But do you know what can't climb a mountain? A skeleton. Sure, there might be a lot of skeletons on Mount Everest today, but I assure you that none of them are walking. If we want to avoid this fate and make it up the mountain with our souls, minds, and spirits intact, we must not miss the critical importance of joy in the journey.

Romans 5:3-4 says, "We *rejoice* in our sufferings, knowing that suffering produces endurance, and endurance produces character, and character produces hope" (emphasis added). These verses suggest that it's not only suffering, but *joy in the midst of suffering*, which produces three essential components in us that we'll need for a successful climb:

1. **<u>ENDURANCE</u>**
   Endurance is what drives us forward, even when all the odds are stacked against us. It's what keeps our legs moving when everything inside of us tells them to quit. Climbing a mountain is hard work, and if we want to have any chance

of making it all the way to the top, we're going to need endurance.

2. **<u>CHARACTER</u>**

Character is the internal compass that directs our decisions on the mountain. I've read that the average person comes up against 35,000 choices per day.[3] Many of these decisions are small and insignificant, having very little impact on what happens on the mountain, but others will be the difference between life and death. And without a compass to guide us in the right direction, we'll put ourselves in unnecessary danger.

3. **<u>HOPE</u>**

Hope is what we cling to when our circumstances betray us. Hope believes that the top of the mountain is still coming, even when it looks like there's no way through. Hope is our last lifeline on the mountain, and if we run out of it, we're done for.

In that sense, hope is perhaps the most essential element of the climb. Orange Kids defines hope as "believing that something good can come out of something bad."[4] And isn't that just what we need on the mountain?

This grueling journey is rarely easy, and things almost never work out the way we planned. Equipment fails, bodies grow tired, weather rages, and feet inevitably begin to slip on precarious paths. But hope always says, "Good will come of this yet."

When it comes to navigating the mountain of life, we'll quickly waste away without endurance, character, and hope. But let's not forget what's at the center of this whole progression: joy.

We were created to experience joy and we don't stand a chance without it. If we don't prioritize joy in times of suffering, our misery will dry up our bones and send us to an early grave. We must not allow a lack of joy to deprive us of the essential equipment we require to complete our mountain journey.

Instead, we must learn to "rejoice in our sufferings." This doesn't mean we have to walk around with fake smiles plastered on our faces, telling our friends that "everything's great" when, really, it's not. But it does mean that we must make intentional decisions every day to choose joy regardless of our circumstances. Because if we don't, the implications are catastrophic.

A CRISIS

According to the World Health Organization, "one in four people in the world will be affected by mental or neurological disorders at some point in their lives."[5] The statistics surrounding mental illness in our world are alarming. In any given year, around one in five people will be affected by a mental health problem or illness in the United States[6] and Canada.[7]

Unfortunately, the statistics don't seem to be any different within the church. In a 2014 study, Lifeway Research showed that 23% of pastors indicated that they had personally suffered from mental illness at some point in their lives.[8]

Now, I'm not a researcher, but I did spend eight and a half years on staff at a North American church. Of the nine full-time staff members on our team, I could identify three individuals (myself included) who struggled openly with mental illness during our time on staff. And those were just the cases I was aware of. The church is not immune to the mental health epidemic we're facing in our world today.

It's natural to think that the global mental health crisis is causing this severe lack of joy. No one experiences joy in the middle of a depressive episode or a panic attack. But I've begun to wonder if it might actually be the other way around. The more I study what the Bible has to say about joy and reflect on the state of our world, the more I wonder if, perhaps, we've arrived at this place as a society because we've neglected the discipline of joy.

Joy in suffering is never natural; it must always be chosen. And choice, by nature, requires discipline. The right decision is often the hard one, and it takes discipline to consistently choose what's wise when easier options so frequently present themselves.

Sorrow is an easier choice than joy. But could it be that, by neglecting to choose joy even in the midst of troubling circumstances, we've crippled ourselves on the mountain of life? Could it be that the lack of joy we see in our culture today is massively contributing to the decline of endurance, character, and hope in the world around us? Could this decline be partially responsible for the devastating effects of mental illness on our society? And within the church, could this explain why so many of us find ourselves in seasons of lukewarm or apathetic Christianity, floundering around for a sense of purpose and peace?

I think we actually have a joy crisis on our hands.

We're living in a society that's so characterized by stress, worry, busyness, and fear, and we don't seem to understand how the removal of joy from our faith experience is affecting not only our ability to trust God but also our ability to grow in endurance, character, and hope. It seems that we've become satisfied with a new kind of status quo in which stress and worry are not only acceptable but entirely conventional, and where it is often seen as an anomaly when a Christian chooses joy and strength in the face of great trials.

Many of us live such safe, comfortable lives in the context of Western Christianity that we rarely ever have the opportunity to suffer for our faith. As a result, we seem to have lost sight of the idea that joy in suffering is a discipline that causes necessary spiritual growth in our lives. Instead, we forfeit that growth for the comfort and control of worry and stress, and we allow our faith in God to become a cheap caricature of what the early church Christians experienced as their faith was tried and tested through persecution and fire.

I believe that now, more than ever, we need a move of the Holy Spirit to restore joy to his people.

A NEW BEGINNING

The time for a new beginning has come. We must not wait any longer. This isn't a problem we can keep putting off until a more convenient time because there's simply too much at stake. We must begin to understand the biblical foundation for joy today so that we can build toward a better tomorrow.

I'm not a mental health professional. Neither do I suppose that within these few short pages I'll be able to single-handedly eradicate the plague of mental illness. But my hope is that, in writing this book, I'll inspire the genesis of a new kind of journey for you, a joy-filled journey up the mountain of life.

That's why I'm writing this book. I'm writing this book as a person who has suffered the devastating effects of a joyless life, who has wrestled with the biblical narrative of joy, and who has found myself and the world around me lacking.

I'm writing this book as a person on the same mountain journey as you. The climb hasn't been easy, and there will be plenty more obstacles to overcome in the days and years ahead. But I don't want to give up. I want to endure through the pain, make characterful decisions, and hold onto hope that something better is coming. Because if I do, I know that I'll be able to reach the top of the mountain with a sense of fulfillment, satisfaction, and gratitude.

And I want that! But I don't just want it for me. I want it for my loved ones, too. I want it for the next generation. I want it for all of you.

But if we're ever going to get there, it's imperative that we uncover the mysteries of joy in the heavenward journey. As a faith community, we have a responsibility to ourselves and to those coming after us to address the joy crisis that's crippling us as Christians. If we don't, we risk leading the next generation into a future devoid of endurance, character, and hope, the effects of which we've already begun to feel today. Fortunately, the problems of today don't have to define the future.

So what are we waiting for? There's a joy revolution lying dormant in the heart of the mountain, just waiting for us to claim it and release it into the world. But it won't be found by dead men walking. So it's time to wake up. It's time to get out of your coffin, put some flesh on those bones, clothe yourself in joy, and join me on this journey up the mountain.

The revolution is now. And where does every good revolution begin?

With a worthy goal.

QUESTIONS FOR REFLECTION

On "The Genesis"

1. Can you see a correlation between joy and the growth of endurance, character, and hope (or the lack thereof) in your own life?

2. How has your life been impacted by the joy crisis facing our world today? How has this crisis affected the people around you?

3. Are you ready for a new beginning? If so, please read on.

CHAPTER 2

The Goal

If you ever plan a trip to Lloydminster, I would recommend against flying.

To be fair, I'm not sure why you would ever plan a trip to Lloydminster. Besides being one of Canada's only border towns, located right on top of the Alberta-Saskatchewan provincial line, it's not exactly a tourist hotspot.

Don't get me wrong; I love the community. It's where I got married, where my daughter Avra was born, and where I spent nearly a decade serving on staff at a local church. But despite the many amazing memories I have made here, I haven't had the best luck when it comes to the Lloydminster Municipal Airport.

When I first moved to Lloydminster in 2010, flying commercially to and from this community wasn't really an option. The nearest airport was a three-hour drive away, meaning that travel was always a hassle. Considering it took ten hours to drive to my parents' home in Manitoba, and twelve hours in the opposite direction to visit my in-laws in Kelowna, BC, I'm sure you can imagine my excitement when a major airline announced it would begin flying to Lloydminster in the summer of 2018!

We didn't have much time available for a family vacation that August, but since we now had the option to fly, my husband and I enthusiastically booked tickets for a quick trip to the Rocky Mountains to visit his parents. It was exciting because we wouldn't have to make the 12-hour drive with an eight-month-old baby who required a nursing stop every few hours, but also because it was a brand-new experience. With commercial flights having just opened up in our city, we were among some of the first people from the general public to fly out of Lloydminster for leisure. We felt like pioneers!

As luck would have it, we continued to feel like pioneers through the duration of that trip because a covered wagon could have carried us to our destination faster. Though we did make it to Kelowna in the end, due to an unimaginable sequence of cancellations and delays, a trip that should have taken us around three hours, ended up lasting over thirty-two! Can you imagine? We have literally flown to Rwanda in less time than that!

Have you ever been on a trip like this? One thing after another goes awry and eventually you are left wondering if this journey is even worth it. It's not so bad at first when you receive the initial delay notification on your phone. Though not ideal, you remind yourself that flights get delayed all the time. At that point you can still reassure yourself that it will all work out, and you go on waiting.

But then the next notification comes in, and then another one. Eventually, after five hours of waiting, you find out that your flight has ultimately been cancelled. With only one flight in and out of that small regional airport every day, you have no choice but to go home and try again tomorrow.

On day two, when you finally do board a plane, you think to yourself, "Okay. We can still salvage this vacation." But after further delays, when you find yourself sprinting at Olympic speed through the next airport with an infant in your arms, only to watch as your connection flight departs from the gate without your family on it, you genuinely start to wonder if any of this is actually happening or if you're living in some kind of morose nightmare.

Sometimes the journey up the mountain of life feels a little bit like that. Even when you think you have your route mapped out, it can change in an instant because of inclement weather or broken equipment. As each leg of the journey becomes increasingly complicated and painful, you find yourself losing steam for the trek ahead. Sometimes you fall and have to make up lost ground. And sometimes the opposition is so intense and discouraging that you want to give up altogether.

This book is here to prevent that. This book is here to tether us together as fellow climbers on the mountain so that we can push each other forward and spur one another on to reach our ultimate goal.

CALLED HEAVENWARD

The apostle Paul, who wrote almost a quarter of the New Testament, was a person who understood this goal. In fact, his life was a powerful example of what it looks like to persevere to the top of the mountain.

In his letter to the church in Philippi, Paul wrote, "I press on to take hold of that for which Christ Jesus took hold of me. Brothers, I do not consider myself yet to have taken hold of it. But one thing I do: Forgetting what is behind and straining toward what is ahead, I press on toward the goal to win the prize for which God has called me heavenward in Christ Jesus" (Phil. 3:12b-14).

Paul was a man on a mission. He was a man who understood the mountain and had surrendered to its Maker. He knew that the mountain was full of twists and turns, unexpected obstacles, and unpredictable conditions. But he refused to give up. Instead he resolved to "press on toward the goal" because he knew exactly where he was going.

Home.

"Our citizenship is in heaven," he encouraged his friends at Philippi (Phil. 3:20). "That's why we've got to keep climbing this mountain. We were called heavenward, invited to a party at the summit. So we can't give up. We can't focus on how hard the journey has been. We just have to keep climbing. We've got to press on toward the goal."

Okay, Paul didn't really say it quite like that. But I think that's what he was getting at. Looking around himself, he observed a world obsessed with the here and now. "Their mind is on earthly things," he said of those he considered "enemies of the cross of Christ" (Phil. 3:18-19). He saw how easy it was for people to get distracted from the ultimate goal.

The mountain path can be gruelling at times, but it also offers scenic rest stops, refreshing streams, and spectacular views along the way. In those places, laziness quickly sets in. After a push of effort to make it that far, many people decide to set up camp and enjoy the comforts of the mountain.

But Paul was reaching for a higher goal. He was convinced that what awaited him at the summit was better than anything the mountain had to offer. And he wasn't going to stop until he got there.

I think Paul was onto something. We're all on a journey home. We progress heavenward as we continue to climb the mountain of life. Now don't misunderstand me; I'm not saying that we climb this mountain to somehow earn our place in heaven. When I say that our goal is to reach the summit, I'm not suggesting that we must strive our way through life to secure our eternal hope. Paul wasn't suggesting that either.

In fact, after telling the Philippians that our true citizenship lies in heaven, in his very next breath, Paul reminded them that "we eagerly await a Savior from there, the Lord Jesus Christ" (Phil. 3:20). He knew we couldn't get there on our own. Reaching the summit isn't about achieving salvation, it's about experiencing the fulfillment of our faith. It's not about the efforts we have exerted, it's about the ending God has established.

Our final deliverance comes when we reach the end of our lives, the top of the mountain, and step into eternity. This is the prize Paul wrote about in Philippians 3:14, and it's the goal of our lives as believers. We want to reach the finish line with a sense of fulfillment and our faith intact.

Paul did just that. "I have fought the good fight, I have finished the race, I have kept the faith," he told Timothy toward the end of his life. "Now there is in store for me the crown of righteousness, which the Lord, the righteous Judge, will award to me on that day—and not only to me, but also to all who have longed for his appearing" (2 Tim. 4:7-8).

Paul fulfilled his purpose. He didn't just wander around aimlessly all over the mountain. He set his sights on the summit and determined that nothing would stop him. He ran "in such a way as to get the prize" (1 Cor. 9:24), a crown of righteousness that would be bestowed upon him by the King himself.

THE KING OF THE MOUNTAIN

Who is this King? And by what means did he ascend the throne? His kingship was not won in battle nor inherited from a long line of monarchs. Rather, he has always been in power. Long before the inception of the mountain, the King reigned over his "everlasting kingdom" (Ps. 145:13).

And this isn't just any old king. He's certainly not unstable and brash like England's King Henry VIII who went through six wives during his time on the throne, two of whom were beheaded by his own orders.[9] Nor is he blindly ignorant like Princess Jasmin's sweet but bumbling father, the Sultan of Agrabah, who managed to get himself hypnotized under Jafar's wicked sorcery.[10]

Of course, not all kings—whether factual or fabled—are tyrannical or oblivious. But even the leaders of this world who are benevolent and wise must still grapple with their human limitations. They're neither all-powerful nor all-knowing, and when faced with crisis must make hard decisions under pressure. In these moments, weaknesses present themselves and corruption finds opportunity to seep through cracks in the foundation. But not with the King of the mountain.

No, the King of the mountain is quite a different kind of King. He's greater than any ruler, president, prime minister, or monarch that our world or imaginations have ever known.

To say he's a good King would be an understatement. He's the perfect King: perfectly merciful and perfectly just. It's easy to set your allegiance to a King like this who is eagerly devoted to the wellbeing of his people. And this is true of our God—the mighty King of the mountain. He's zealously committed to our highest good.

What's more, he actually likes us! After all, he's not only our King but also our Maker. And like a smitten parent who relishes every moment and milestone in their child's life, Psalm 149:4 says that "the Lord takes delight in his people." We make God smile by simply being who we were created to be.

A CROWN

"The Lord takes delight in his people; he crowns the humble with salvation" (Ps. 149:4).

There's that word "crown" again. What other king not only allows his followers to wear a crown along with him, but actually crafts and designs it specifically for them? A royal crown distinguishes a king and sets him apart from his subjects. But we have a King who takes this royal marker, this symbol of honor, glory, and power, and eagerly prepares to bestow it on us when our homecoming journey is complete.

There's a crown waiting at the summit for all of us, and the way we live our lives on the mountain determines whether or not we'll receive it. Again, please don't misinterpret my meaning. This isn't about striving to live a perfect life. This is about surrendering to a perfect God.

I love the way Romans 5:2 in the New Living Translation puts it: "Because of our faith, Christ has brought us into this place of undeserved privilege where we now stand, and we confidently and joyfully look forward to sharing God's glory."

The fact that we can participate in a real relationship with the King of the mountain in the first place is an undeserved privilege. We can't climb the social ladder high enough to position ourselves in his presence, nor can we do enough good to earn his favor. The fact is that our sinful, selfish natures cause us to come up short every single time and disqualify us from any kind of glory (Rom. 3:23).

Yet, the heroic feats of our mighty Warrior Prince have brought us into this place of undeserved privilege. We'll talk more about him in the next chapter, but for now, we can know that because of the great victory he won on our behalf, his Father, the King, invites us into his presence to share in his glory.

If there was ever a reason for unspeakable joy, this is it! As Christ's followers, we have the advantage of navigating the gruelling journey up the mountain with a hope that changes everything! We know that once we've fought the good fight, run the race, and kept the faith, we'll be brought into God's glorious presence and adorned with a royal crown that we didn't earn, but that we'll get to keep for all of eternity (1 Cor. 9:25).

Imagine that moment. Battered and bruised, exhausted and worn from an excruciating journey that felt endless at times, you hurl your aching body forward in one final thrust. The summit.

In an instant, everything changes. The aches and pains are gone, and so is the weight of the heavy pack you've been carrying all this time. Moments ago, you were on the verge of hypothermia, dragging yourself up the frozen, snowy peak. Now you feel warm—the rich, cozy kind of warm that you felt as a child when you curled up by the fireplace on Christmas Eve or put on fresh pajamas straight out of the dryer.

What is this place? you wonder as you blink your eyes, adjusting to the dazzling light.

At first you think it's just the bright, unhindered sun reflecting off the snow, but then you realize that it can't be. The snow is gone. In fact, so is the mountain.

You find your feet now on something shiny and gold. And that's what everything seems to be here: gold, all glistening in the light of... where is that light coming from, anyway?

As everything comes into focus, your heart begins to race.

It's him!

At last you understand. The source of the light, now moving majestically in your direction, is the King himself! And he's walking toward you with something round and regal in his hands. A crown. Your crown!

And in that moment, all of the hardships you experienced over all those years as you were climbing down below are swept away into the distant past. None of it matters now. You have fought the good fight. You have run your race. You have kept the faith. And you have received your crown.

A RESPONSE AND A RESPONSIBILITY

Paul lived for this moment. This picture, or some variation of it, is what enabled him to forget the past and strain toward the goal for which God had called him heavenward (Phil. 3:13-14). It's what kept him going through appalling circumstances and compelled him to choose joy through unimaginable sorrow.

See, Paul understood that joy is both a response and a responsibility. He recognized that without it, he would never develop the endurance needed to make it all the way to the summit. So, despite his circumstances, he *chose* to live a life of radical joy.

In 2 Corinthians 6:10, after publishing a laundry list of hardships that he and his companions frequently endured, Paul declared that he was "sorrowful, yet always rejoicing." These guys had plenty of reasons for sorrow. Just look at the list in 2 Corinthians 6:4-5. Troubles, hardships, distresses, beatings, imprisonments, riots, hard work, sleepless nights, and hunger were the difficulties they faced day in and day out.

Paul's ministry team wasn't staying in cushy hotels or eating fancy dinners. They were going hungry. They were enduring sleepless nights. They were victims of violence and religious hate crimes. They had every reason to be sorrowful, yet they rejoiced! In fact, they were *full* of joy because they knew there was a crown coming. They had fixed their eyes on the goal.

As believers, we all have a responsibility to do the same. Every day, we're faced with all kinds of choices about how we'll react and respond to the circumstances around us. Will we surrender to our circumstances and let sorrow overtake us? Or will we, like Paul, overcome them by choosing a life of radical joy?

Joy is a response, but it's not a response to our circumstances. Real, genuine, unspeakable joy can never be a direct response to our circumstances because circumstances are always changing. Sometimes, they're good, but let's face it, the circumstances we encounter on the mountain of life are frequently difficult and draining. If we go through life allowing joy to be a response to our circumstances, we'll largely forfeit our ability to experience any joy at all.

Paul and his companions were "sorrowful, yet always rejoicing." But when I look around at Western Christianity today, I struggle to find this lifestyle demonstrated in individual lives. Sometimes I wonder if a more accurate description of our current reality would be "blessed, yet always sorrowful," the exact opposite of the attitude that Paul modeled and preached. So many of us live in both physical and spiritual plenty today, yet we allow unfavorable circumstances to blind us to our own blessings.

Frankly, even when we find ourselves in the midst of economic downturns, job instability, relational brokenness, global pandemics, or any other challenges we may face, the reality is that we're still profoundly blessed because of the hope of the gospel. But when we choose to live as "blessed, yet always sorrowful," we diminish the freedom that Jesus died for us to experience.

COURSE CORRECTION

Now, please don't let your heart be discouraged. Yes, this is a heavy, convicting truth, and most of us come up on the wrong side of it more often than not. But along with this hard truth, I want to offer a powerfully redeeming message to lighten the load.

All of us get off course sometimes on the mountain of life. If you have been living as "blessed, yet always sorrowful," it's safe to say that you might have missed a few critical turns along the mountain path. But as long as you're alive, it's not too late to course correct.

In her TEDx Talk titled, *Lessons from the Ledge*,[11] mountaineer Alison Levine shared what it was like to turn around and begin her final descent when she was only a few hundred feet away from reaching the summit on her first trek up Mount Everest. At that altitude, such a short distance would have taken a few hours to travel because of the extra effort required to simply breathe. But when a storm rolled in as her team prepared to crest the mountain, she knew she needed to make a hard call.

"Turning around and walking away from the deal is harder than continuing on," Levine admitted. "But when you're up there in these mountains you have to be able to make very tough decisions when the conditions around you are far from perfect."

On the mountain of life, we too must come prepared to make some tough calls when we find that the conditions we face aren't conducive to reaching our goal. "Blessed, yet always sorrowful" is a great example of such conditions. No matter how much ground we've covered on the journey so far, this detrimental mindset will eventually turn into a raging storm before we ever reach the summit.

When that happens, we always find ourselves between a rock and a hard place, just like Alison Levine did as she gazed upon the pinnacle of Mount Everest, weighing the threat of the storm ahead against the months of hard work behind her.

But like Levine, we're also presented with a choice. Do we push forward at the risk of great personal danger to ourselves and the people around us? Or do we humbly consider the cost and make the hard decision to course correct as needed?

Sometimes, a course correction is as simple as taking a small step to the side in order to avoid a dangerous pitfall. Other times, it means turning around completely and descending to a place where you can catch your breath, get your bearings, and reassess your route.

We will face many moments on the mountain of life when a course correction is required. In these moments, our true character is put on display. Will we take responsibility for our actions, recognize where we went wrong, and then take the necessary steps to correct our behavior? Or will we refuse to admit that we made some bad judgment calls and find ourselves right in the middle of a storm?

When the latter is true, many times, we're too proud to turn back and course correct. Though we wind up all alone on the most treacherous of terrain, having lost our gear and guide along the way, we'll tell ourselves anything to justify our decisions and drive us forward, regardless of the cost.

Some of the most devastating fatalities on the mountain happen this way. But not when we're willing to course correct.

Perhaps, like me, you're realizing that it's time for a major course correction in the area of "blessed, yet always sorrowful." As I've searched my own heart over this issue, I've come to the decisive conclusion that it's unacceptable for me to live in the context of such abundant and lavish blessing, yet to consistently choose sorrow over joy.

As a follower of Christ, I have a responsibility to take my eyes off myself and off the mountain and to fix them firmly instead on the King and the crown. Because when I do that, I'm empowered to choose "sorrowful, yet always rejoicing." When I do that, I activate a well-oiled machine that takes joy and turns it into endurance, character, and hope.

FREE FOR THE TAKING

Still, if the idea of "sorrowful, yet always rejoicing" makes you cower in your boots a little bit or, worse yet, want to give up on this book altogether, please stick with me. Remember, I've been where you are. I've stood facing the impossible mountain of joy, buckling under the onerous burden of what it takes to reach the top.

But don't forget that joy is not the mountain we're aiming to climb! Even if you feel that you could never climb very high on the mountain of joy, rest assured that you certainly can on the mountain of life. And I'll show you how within the pages of this book.

But if we're going to make it up the mountain, if we want to have any hope of reaching our goal, we must discover how to embrace joy in a world that robustly rejects it. This world tells us that happiness is all about momentary comforts and self-serving pleasures. But we know better.

We know that joy cannot be bought for the price of a new house or a fancy car. It's not a commodity that can be traded or sold. It cannot be negotiated for by the most adept lawyers or won fair and square by the world's greatest athlete.

Quite the contrary, joy is free for the taking for anyone who wants it. But it has to be chosen. It must come with an attitude that says, "Life isn't all about me and my circumstances." It's about pressing on "to take hold of that for which Christ Jesus took hold of me" (Phil. 3:12). It's about radical salvation for all people.

As Paul rounds out his thoughts in 2 Corinthians 6:10, in addition to "sorrowful, yet always rejoicing," he shares that he is "poor, yet making many rich; having nothing, and yet possessing everything." When we understand the goal of the mountain, we begin to realize that we are unimaginably rich. We are heirs in the eternal kingdom, on our way home to receive our crowns! This, in and of itself, should be enough to elicit profound joy!

But to add some icing to the cake, we have the opportunity to share our riches with others when we bring them along on the journey with us. There's no such thing as keeping the crown all for ourselves, so we needn't worry about that. There are enough crowns to go around! Hoarding our claim to the crown will only lose it for us in the end.

Instead, the King invites us into his mission and adventure. As we climb the mountain, poor as we may be, he invites us to make many rich—to share the story and point others heavenward—and, in so doing, to realize that we have everything we need.

And that's a guarantee.

QUESTIONS FOR REFLECTION

On "The Goal"

1. What are the goals that motivate you in life? Do these goals line up with the biblical mandate to fight the good fight, finish the race, and keep the faith (2 Tim. 4:7)?

2. Which of these two phrases better describes your life: "sorrowful, yet always rejoicing," or "blessed, yet always sorrowful"?

3. What hard decisions do you need to make today to correct your course on the mountain of life?

CHAPTER 3

The Guarantee

In 1944, Japanese intelligence officer Hiroo Onoda[12] was sent on mission to a remote Philippine island to carry out guerilla warfare during the second world war. Unfortunately, despite several attempts to get the message out, Onoda was never officially informed that the war came to an end in 1945. So, devoted to his country and determined to carry out his war orders, he remained hidden under the cover of the jungle. When leaflets and search parties went out to notify him of Japan's surrender, Onoda dismissed them as nothing more than a strategic ploy of the enemy.

Weeks turned into months, months turned into years, and Onoda steadfastly refused to surrender. Eventually, after twenty-nine years of surviving off bananas and coconuts and carrying out his war orders in denial, his former commander was flown in from Japan to see him and to issue a direct order that all combat activity cease.

Twenty-nine years. Let that sink in. For nearly three decades, this tenacious soldier hid in the jungle fighting a war that had long since ended. Many other wars and global conflicts began and ended within that time.

It's hard to fathom such an outlandish story. But when it comes down to it, many of us have more in common with Mr. Onoda than we'd like to admit. The truth is that we're living in a time of spiritual victory today, yet so many of us conduct ourselves on the mountain as though we're living in a time of war.

War times are times of suffering, rations, and fear. They're times when you hide in your basement to protect yourself and you must constantly watch over your shoulder to make sure you're safe. You can't walk around freely in the streets because your oppressors are there on every corner, always ready to attack. Every day, you wake up wondering if you'll make it to tomorrow. Then, even if you do, you live in perpetual fear, knowing that the war being waged around you could end in the definitive loss of your freedom and future.

But this is not the spiritual reality we're living in today. As we make our way up the mountain, we don't have to wonder about our future or fate. We don't have to live under the oppression of insecurity, depression, anxiety, addictions, or fear. We don't have to live in bondage to sin.

Yet, so many of us do. So many of us trudge along the mountain path as though we're prisoners of war, dragging a ball and chain behind us. Over time, we become so accustomed to captivity that we cannot accept freedom.

THE WAR FOR THE MOUNTAIN

To be clear, a war *has* taken place. Indeed, a great war for our salvation has been fought and won on the battlefield of the mountain. But to understand this war, we must travel all the way back to the beginning.

There was nothing then. Not a rock, not a plant, not the faintest sound of a trickling mountain stream. Nothing that we know of the mountain had yet come into existence. But the King and his court were there, along with his brilliant designs for the world we now know.

And then, with a single breath, the King spoke and suddenly there in the void stood a great and majestic mountain. The mountain of life.

Adorned with all of the splendor of his own beauty and illuminated by the shining glory of the King himself, the mountain was the perfect home for the crown of his creation: us. Humankind was born, handcrafted in such a way to bear his image and carry his royal seal on our hearts.

It sounds like paradise, and it was. Until a banished member of the King's court came around with an agenda of his own. This insidious enemy, embittered by the blameless benevolence and impenetrable power of the King, became hellbent on bringing ruin to the mountain and all who lived there. So, he cast a dark shadow over the mountain, separating the people from the glorious light of their King and forcing them to wander around in darkness, unable to make out the pathway home.

They can't climb the mountain in the dark, the enemy thought. But the King was far from defeated. What the enemy planned as a surprise invasion of the mountain kingdom, the King had seen coming from miles away. And he had a plan of his own.

Eager to secure the fate of his beloved people, the King sent a great Warrior down the mountain to defeat the powers of darkness. A prince in his own right, this Warrior gladly accepted the rank of a commoner in order to accomplish the great mission for which he'd been sent.

And that he did. Beginning at its very base and carrying the weight of the world on his back, the Prince began his ascent up the mountain. Attacked on every side by the usurping enemy, the Prince fought his way through the darkness with one single goal: reach the summit. He knew that his summit bid—a feat that no other man could achieve on his own—was the key to lifting the darkness and reuniting the mountain with the brilliant light of the King.

So onward and upward was his course, despite the treacherous conditions the mountain threw at him. And there, in the final moments of the battle, it almost seemed as if all hope was lost. Broken, battered, and panting for oxygen, the Prince gave everything he had to that mission, even down to his very last breath.

Crumbling to the ground as his feet hit the summit and his life slipped away, he reached out and pulled down the curtain of darkness in one final heroic feat. This mighty Warrior had defeated the darkened mountain, along with the oppressive pretender to the throne who claimed to be its ruler, sealing the kingdom with a guarantee of freedom for all of eternity.

The Prince of Peace, as this great hero of war came to be known, had won the victory. And what awaited him at the summit? A crown. The very same crown that he won for each and every one of us. And not only a crown of righteousness, displaying the perfect blamelessness and morality with which he waged war on the kingdom of darkness, but also a crown of life.

"Blessed is the one who perseveres under trial because, having stood the test, that person will receive the crown of life that the Lord has promised to those who love him" (James 1:12).

Jesus was the first to take hold of this crown of life. Having conquered the mountain under the shroud of darkness, he was crowned with everlasting life, even after death. And this resurgence of life is the fate he sealed for each and every one of us who choose to follow his course and climb the mountain in his footsteps.

THE DECEIVER

Today, we live in the victory of our mighty Prince of Peace. In the cosmic battle for our souls, Jesus came out on top. Though we were once subjects in a kingdom of darkness, we have now been delivered into a kingdom of light. And there's no need to walk around afraid of our oppressors in this kingdom because we have a good King who cannot be dethroned.

This, however, is not what the enemy would have us believe. Satan wants us to believe that we're still living in war times. And if he can trick us into thinking that we're still at war, then we'll never let our guard down to walk in the freedom that Jesus already won for us. So, what does he do? He scurries around on the mountain selling us cheap lies to keep us from pursuing the goal.

Picture one of those shady merchants in a fairy tale who sets up his wagon on the side of the road, waiting for unsuspecting travelers to wander by and peruse his supply of phony elixirs.

"Trying to climb the mountain?" he'll ask in a slippery voice. "Why, I've got just the thing for you. Come and have a look."

You feel a twinge of suspicion inside as he beckons you over to his merchant cart, but you can't seem to shake your curiosity. After a compelling presentation, you've bought into the lies and swallowed the potion. He promised it would make you stronger, braver, faster. But as you head out on your way, the only thing that changes is that, strangely, nightfall comes too soon.

Or is it night? It almost looks as if the sun is still shining, but ever so faintly behind a dark, shadowy haze. Is this supposed to be happening? Dizzy and confused, you turn around to look for that merchant, but he's gone without a trace. So, there you stand, disoriented and bewildered, trying to remember what you were doing in the first place.

Satan is a master deceiver and the king of all lies. As you've already read, one of his tactics in my life was to convince me that the mountain went by a different name: the mountain of joy. He persuaded me to believe that joy was only possible if I could reach the summit, a lie just big enough to discourage me from ever trying. And here's one thing I know: If the deceiver can steal our joy, he can keep us stuck on the mountain until it kills us.

Remember, joy is essential in the journey of life because joy in the midst of suffering, which abounds on the mountain, is what produces endurance, then character, then hope. And why attack all three when he could simply target the root?

Satan is committed to stealing our joy, because he knows it will thwart our progress on the mountain. He will go after it by any means necessary simply to spit in the face of the King he despises. The great war is over, and he has been defeated fair and square, but this vindictive, conniving cheat is on a mission to make sure we don't know it. Why? Because if we truly grasp and embrace our freedom and victory in Jesus, our joy will be unstoppable.

GRIEF IN ALL KINDS OF TRIALS

Consider the words of the apostle Peter:

> [3]Praise be to the God and Father of our Lord Jesus Christ! In his great mercy he has given us new birth into a living hope through the resurrection of Jesus Christ from the dead, [4]and into an inheritance that can never perish, spoil or fade. This inheritance is kept in heaven for you, [5]who through faith are shielded by God's power until the coming of the salvation that is ready to be revealed in the last time. [6]In all this you greatly rejoice, though now for a little while you may have had to suffer grief in all kinds of trials. [7]These have come so that the proven genuineness of your faith—of greater worth than gold, which perishes even though refined by fire—may result in praise, glory and honor when Jesus Christ is revealed. [8]Though you have not seen him, you love him; and even though you do not see him now, you believe in him and are filled with

an ***inexpressible and glorious joy***, [9]for you are
receiving the end result of your faith, the salvation
of your souls. (1 Pet. 1:3-9, emphasis added)

Did you catch that? Inexpressible and glorious joy! This kind of
joy infuriates our enemy. It poses a serious threat to his mission to
keep us all stuck on the mountain. But he knows that when we have
our eyes fixed on the goal and we cling to the truth that there's an
inheritance that cannot perish, spoil, or fade being kept at the summit
for us, glorious, inexpressible joy will be much easier to come by.

So, the deceiver gets to work. And when God's word says, "In all
this you greatly rejoice," Satan surreptitiously diverts our attention to
the second half of this verse which says, "though now for a little while
you may have had to suffer grief in all kinds of trials" (1 Pet. 1:6).

After all, everyone can relate to that part. In fact, that part is so
real to us that it almost feels as if Peter was sugarcoating it when he
said that we *may* have to suffer through some grief and trials for a
little while.

Seriously, Peter? This is exactly how my husband approaches
me when he wants me to agree to something that he knows I'm not
going to be in favor of! To soften the blow, he'll start out by saying,
"So hear me out…" But as soon as I hear those words, I know it's all
downhill from there!

In some ways, it feels like that's exactly what Peter is doing here
with the second half of verse 6. I kind of wish he would just tell it like
it is! Why doesn't he just come right out and say that on the mountain
we'll suffer all kinds of grief, all the time, for the rest of our lives?
No matter how committed we are to our goal or how arduously we
cling to joy in the journey, the reality is that climbing the mountain
is really hard. Life just isn't all that forgiving.

And that's what Satan wants. He wants us to busy ourselves
focusing on the suffering and the grief so that we can forget all about

the inexpressible joy. Our adversary knows exactly what Peter meant in verse 6 when he said, "In all this you greatly rejoice," but he doesn't want us to see it. Because if we can unlock the meaning behind "in all this," Satan knows we'll release an overflow of joy.

So let's do that.

IN ALL THIS

If you're anything like me, the phrase "in all this you greatly rejoice" brings up more questions than it does answers. First, I read it and think that Peter has got this all wrong because I don't feel like I am greatly rejoicing at all. I'm stressed, I'm tired, and I'm maybe even a bit grumpy. Secondly, even if I felt like I *could* greatly rejoice, I still don't know what "in all this" means. In all *what*, Peter? In all *what* do you want me to rejoice?

If you're *not* anything like me, right now you're probably thinking, *Calm down, Talasi.* (And that's pronounced TA-la-see, by the way. It rhymes with fallacy and is basically the same word as Tallahassee, without the "ha." I'm telling you this now because I've spent my whole life being called ta-LASSIE, like the dog, and feeling too timid to correct people. No matter how well I fake it, the truth is that I'm undeniably an introvert who struggles hopelessly with first impressions! I know if I were to meet you in person and have you mispronounce my name, I would awkwardly let it slide and have you call me ta-LASSIE for the next few years until eventually someone else corrected you, leaving you feeling embarrassed and ashamed for associating me with America's favorite dog. And I don't want that for you.)

So now that we've got that out of the way, please continue. "Calm down, Talasi," you were saying. "Peter explained it all in verses 3 through 5."

Thank you for talking me down off that ledge, friend. Let's review this passage and have a look together.

> [3]Praise be to the God and Father of our Lord Jesus Christ! In his great mercy he has given us new birth into a living hope through the resurrection of Jesus Christ from the dead, [4]and into an inheritance that can never perish, spoil or fade. This inheritance is kept in heaven for you, [5]who through faith are shielded by God's power until the coming of the salvation that is ready to be revealed in the last time. [6]In all this you greatly rejoice, though now for a little while you may have had to suffer grief in all kinds of trials. (1 Pet. 1:3-6)

In verse 3, Peter says that God, in his great mercy, chose to give us new life and fresh hope—hope that is alive through the resurrection of Jesus. In other words, he points to the crown of life that the Prince of Peace won when he conquered the mountain and reminds us that this gift is available for all who follow him.

He goes on to say in verse 4 that this hope, this promised crown, can never perish, spoil, or fade. When we choose to follow the path of his victorious Son, the great and mighty King of the mountain writes us into the royal will, sealing our inheritance forever.

Finally, in verse 5 we see that even now as we navigate the mountain path, challenging and trying as it may be, our fate is protected and promised by our faith and by the power of God at work in us. And suddenly, we're no longer striving only toward a goal, but also toward a guarantee.

As we make our way back to verse 6, these few simple words somehow become much clearer. In all *this* you greatly rejoice. All of the above are reasons for a joy that transcends suffering, grief, and all kinds of terrible circumstances. In fact, joy is not a response to our circumstances at all. Rather, joy is a response to the guaranteed inheritance awaiting us at the summit.

And this inheritance is not like any of the good things that we have in this life. Because even the very best things in life can be lost. Even the most wonderful events on the mountain can become a source of heartache and disappointment.

When my husband and I found out that I was pregnant with our second baby, we were ecstatic. We told all of our family and close friends right away because we couldn't keep our joy to ourselves… until we went for an early ultrasound at what we understood to be the nine-week mark of this pregnancy. But what our ultrasound technician found, instead, was that I had miscarried, and my body didn't even know it yet.

Up until this moment, in my mind, I was over two months pregnant. I had taken two pregnancy tests, one at home and one at the doctor's clinic, and both came back positive. I felt pregnant. My body was full of pregnancy hormones, I was exhausted, and I was becoming more and more unsettled at the sight of food every day. All the signs were there. There was no doubt in my mind that I was pregnant.

But not according to that ultrasound. According to that ultrasound, there was no baby. Talk about something that can perish, spoil, or fade. I went from knowing that I was pregnant in one moment—from celebrating, making plans, and organizing my world to accommodate an addition to the family—to realizing in the next moment that I was no longer carrying a tiny life.

It was devastating.

But what is joy? Joy is a response and a responsibility. It's about something so much bigger than my circumstances, something that cannot perish, spoil, or fade. Joy is a response to my eternal security in Jesus, which is the one thing in this world that cannot let me down.

NOW FOR A LITTLE WHILE

I know I poked some fun at him earlier, but the truth is that I think Peter was onto something when he said that "Now for a little while" we would face the hardships of the mountain. Because he got the fact that it would be temporary. It might feel as if he were sugarcoating it for us, but he was actually just describing our reality.

Peter knew that the war was over. He experienced Jesus' death. He saw the resurrected Jesus. He watched Jesus ascend into heaven. This guy was fully aware that a significant victory had been won on our behalf. So why is he talking about trials and battles when he knows that the war is over?

Because he also knows that we live in a fallen, broken world. He knows that there is an awkward tension between the victory that Jesus won for us and the "not yet" of the coming kingdom of heaven. He knows that our experience here and now on the mountain doesn't entirely match the fullness of the victory that was won on the summit.

Think of it this way. There's always a mess to clean up after a great battle. Just picture any superhero movie you've ever seen. These movies are riddled with epic battle scenes that happen in city streets, around prestigious buildings, and in the most prominent places of the world. Walls are busted through, fires spring up out of nowhere, vehicles get thrown around, and buildings collapse! It's a colossal mess.

But haven't you ever thought about what happens when it's all over? We never see that part in the movie. The storyline just carries on as though nothing ever happened, and we're left wondering who's going to clean up all that mess.

We know that war destroys things and creates a whole lot of rubble. Sometimes there are people trapped inside that rubble waiting for someone to come along and set them free. And isn't this, in a sense, our mission as believers as we follow the great Warrior up the mountain? The victory is sealed, but there's still work to be done.

This, of course, creates a golden opportunity for the shady merchant to sell us another pack of lies. Satan sees the fact that there's still work to be done and twists the truth to convince us that the war isn't over when it truly is. He's got his army of minions out there running around and wreaking havoc on our lives while we're exposed and vulnerable, working to pick up the pieces.

He capitalizes on our weak wills and gullibility to persuade us that our suffering means we're not really free at all. He'll try to convince you that he still owns the mountain and that you'll never make it out of here alive; that this depression, this divorce, this miscarriage, this season of suffering, this battle that you're fighting right now is a done deal. You can't win. There's no way out, so you might as well give up now.

But back to Peter's words. "Now for a little while."

Our suffering won't last forever. Even if it lasts until the end of our earthly lives, which it might—Jesus never promised otherwise—we know that this suffering will pale in comparison to the inheritance that's coming for those whose faith is in Jesus.

And remember, this inheritance isn't a maybe. It's not like those Forever Sharp knives my husband bought for his mom years ago after a very convincing Costco salesman twisted his rubber arm. I mean, come on. No knife can be *truly* forever sharp. But our eternity is forever sealed. It cannot be lost. It cannot be taken away. It cannot die. Because Jesus won the war.

That's where joy comes from. It's embracing the reality that no matter what circumstances you face in this lifetime, no matter what hardships you suffer on the mountain, your fate and your future is secure.

INEXPRESSIBLE JOY

Peter goes on to say in verse 7 that "these [trials] have come so that the proven genuineness of your faith—of greater worth than gold, which perishes even though refined by fire—may result in praise, glory, and honor when Jesus Christ is revealed" (1 Pet. 1:7).

When it comes to the trials and tribulations we face on the mountain, if there's one thing I know they do, it's that they prove the genuineness of our faith. It's one thing to subscribe to the hard teachings of Jesus when you're reading them from the comfort of your couch while sipping a mug of chai tea. But it's something else altogether to follow the hard teachings of Jesus when the rubber meets the road, and the mountain deals you some brutal blows, and you have to figure out how to choose joy in the midst of it.

Because joy is more than just a response. Joy is also a responsibility. And unfortunately, joy is still a responsibility when life sucks. Just because it feels like there's a battle raging around us, doesn't mean that we should be living like Hiroo Onoda who hid in the jungle for three decades, not accepting the fact that the war was over and that there was already peace. Instead, we have a responsibility to choose to abandon our mountain hideouts and walk forward in the freedom of the Lord.

And that's why it's so important for us to remember verses 8 and 9.

"Though you have not seen him, you love him; and even though you do not see him now, you believe in him and are filled with an *inexpressible* and glorious joy, for you are receiving the end result of your faith, the salvation of your souls" (1 Pet. 1:8-9, emphasis added).

Don't miss that word, "inexpressible"!

What a remarkable descriptor. Few times in my life have I felt joy that's inexpressible. But this is how the Bible says we should respond to God's mercy and the guarantee of our inheritance! The magnificence of it should eclipse all else in our lives—all struggles, trials, and hardships—because we know the end of this story.

We can have inexpressible joy on the journey, despite the enemy's futile attacks, because we know that Jesus has won the ultimate victory. We know where we're going. We know the destination. Here and now, the mountain path might look hazy and confusing. Some days, it might even look impossible. But no matter what we face, we can trust in the guarantee.

And better yet, we can follow the guide.

QUESTIONS FOR REFLECTION

On "The Guarantee"

1. What battles are you still fighting that Jesus has already won?

2. What comes to mind when you read the phrase "inexpressible joy"? Does this kind of joy seem realistic or improbable to you? Why?

3. How would your life look different if you were to walk more confidently in the guaranteed freedom that Jesus won for you?

CHAPTER 4

The Guide

Have you ever heard of a place called the "death zone"?

With a name like that, you might not believe me if I told you that hundreds of people go there voluntarily every year. But it's true!

In mountaineering, the "death zone" refers to altitudes above 8,000 meters where the human body begins to shut down due to lack of sufficient oxygen. Our bodies function best at sea level, but at 8,848 meters above sea level, Mount Everest poses a severe risk to climbers who wish to brave the summit.[13]

The window of time one can survive in the death zone is minimal at best. You won't find climbers curling up by a fire and settling in for the night at the peak of Mount Everest. In an interview with *Business Insider*, mountaineer Vanessa O'Brien revealed that climbing in the death zone is like "a ticking time bomb of what you really need, maybe 24 hours, up and out. Anything over that, you really risk heading to a memorial at the bottom of the mountain."[14]

Many people climb with supplemental oxygen at these heights, but even then, it's not enough to simulate sea level. Nonetheless, whether you're breathing in canned air or not, when you climb at an altitude that cannot sustain human life, the physical and mental challenges of the mountain become that much more deadly.

THE DEATH ZONE

The war hero of our story had a death zone of his own to withstand as he approached the summit of the great mountain. And, resting at the high camp in those final moments before embarking on the last and most brutal leg of his journey, the Warrior Prince cried out to the King with a plea for pardon.

"Mightn't there be any other way?" he humbly appealed to the King, already knowing full well what answer would follow. There wasn't another way. This was the only way. Our mighty Warrior would have to endure the death zone.

And just like the hundreds of men and women who brave the summit of Everest every single year, this Warrior was already aware of the unique hardships that awaited him in the final hours of his climb. He knew how much physical and mental strain he would have to endure there as he made his final summit push. But contrary to the dangers of Everest, our Warrior intuitively sensed that on his journey, the coming temptation to give up and walk away would be much deadlier than the climb itself.

Knowing what was ahead, the great Warrior had already gathered his closest friends together for one last meal. In this intimate setting, he began to reveal the ultimate plan. He told them that he was about to begin his final ascent up into the death zone and that once he reached the summit, he wouldn't be coming back, at least, not right away. Moreover, he explained that his summit push would be a solo trek and that where he was going, they couldn't follow until later. He had to complete the mission first.

That was the thing. The great Warrior knew that if he didn't summit the mountain and defeat the darkness that cloaked those icy highlands first, no one coming after him would ever be able to reach the goal. He also knew that until he went up the mountain to complete his mission, the Guide would not be able to come down and execute the rest of the plan.

See, while on the mountain, the Warrior Prince had amassed a following of climbers who were eager to learn about the Maker of the mountain. They watched and listened intently as the Prince told stories and demonstrated the character of his Father, the great King. But the plan had never been for the Prince to stay there forever as their teacher, showing them step-by-step the way up the mountain. No, the plan was always that he would go on ahead into the death zone to defeat the darkness and for the Guide to return and lead the climbers home.

PARTING WORDS

In what is commonly known as the "Farewell Discourse" (John 13:31-17:26), a conversation that took place around the table following the last supper, Jesus spoke candidly to his disciples about the things to come. Knowing he wouldn't be with them much longer, he wanted to leave them with some parting wisdom.

"As the Father has loved me, so have I loved you. Now remain in my love. If you keep my commands, you will remain in my love, just as I have kept my Father's commands and remain in his love" (John 15:9-10).

Nestled among the final words that Jesus shared with his followers was this profound instruction to remain in his love. His desire was simply for us to live the way we were created and designed to live: a life aligned with the loving heart of God. With Jesus going on to complete the task before him, we would be the ones to carry on his legacy of love.

But how could we do it? Without him here to remind us what this should look like day in and day out, how could we possibly manage to remain in his love? Well, according to John 15:10, the first step to remaining in Jesus' love is to keep his commands.

Let me put it this way.

I'm terrible at bowling. You might feel like you have whiplash right now from how quickly we jumped from the Bible to the bowling alley... but hear me out. To be successful at the bowling alley, your ball must remain on the lane and out of the gutter. This can be a difficult task to accomplish for a person like me who has around the same level of skill as a blind parrot when it comes to throwing a bowling ball.

I hate to admit it, but the only kind of bowling I'm cut out for is bumper bowling. Now that's a different story altogether! Keeping your ball inside the lane isn't difficult at all when you have a set of bumpers blocking off the gutters.

Remaining in the love of Jesus is a little bit like my bowling experience; it's nearly impossible without a set of bumpers to keep you in line. Luckily, in life, we have a set of bumpers available to us at all times: God's commands. When we walk in obedience to the word of God, we can't get off track and fall into the gutter.

But when we try to do things in our own way, everything starts to derail. It doesn't matter if it happens instantly after an embarrassingly bad throw (which is typically the case when I bowl), or gradually over time as the ball travels down the lane. A bowling ball still cannot score if it winds up in the gutter. Likewise, we lose all hope of remaining in the love of Jesus when we choose not to keep his commands.

But even though the bumpers are available, there's still the element of choice. I'm too proud to go to the bowling alley and ask for the bumper lane, even though I need it. And quite frankly, this is how a lot of us treat Jesus' commands.

Every day, we have the word of God at our disposal to help us remain in Christ's love, but we're often too stubborn to apply it. Instead, we keep hurling bowling balls haphazardly down that

42-inch-wide by 60-foot-long strip of wood with no bumpers in place and wonder why they all keep ending up in the gutter.

Let's be real here. Following Jesus' commands is incredibly hard to do in real life. To begin with, many times we don't even understand how his commands pertain to the specifics of our daily experience. But then, after we decipher their application to our particular set of circumstances, we still have to do the hard work of acting upon them.

This often requires more effort than any of us want to expend. The climb is difficult enough as it is; we don't want to risk losing any of our comforts or safety nets just to try out a different strategy, even if it might be better in the long run. Also, there's still the issue of that shady merchant on the loose who is constantly running around trying to sell us another pack of lies.

When it comes right down to it, we're notoriously bad at navigating the mountain alone. This is why we need the Guide.

FROM ABOVE

The Guide has been hovering over the mountain since its foundations were laid. It's not as if he just leapt into action the moment the Prince reached the summit because now, after several millennia of doing nothing, he finally had some work to do. No, he's been here all along, at work in different ways at different times, but always invested in helping climbers reach the goal.

Even the Warrior Prince leaned heavily on the Guide during his ascent up the mountain. It was by the Guide's power, in fact, that our Prince was able to best the beast and come out victorious in those final moments of the great battle.

After all, the Guide knows all the secrets of the mountain. He was there when the mountain was formed, and he has seen every last inch of it. From the grand, flowing waterfalls down below to the strong, stony peaks above, the Guide knows it all. And because he knows it all, he's our best chance at reaching the summit.

In his unfinished classic, *Mount Analogue*, French writer and poet René Daumal articulated that "what is above knows what is below, but what is below does not know what is above."[15] While Daumal was referring to climbers who have summited a mountain and returned with a deeper knowledge of the world around them, we can aptly apply this profound statement to our experience on the mountain of life.

On this mountain, none of us have yet seen the world from the summit. Often, we suppose we've seen enough to understand what's going on and rationalize our point of view, but the fact remains that we don't have access to the big picture.

Our Guide, on the other hand, does. He's been up and down the mountain a million times. He himself was the breath of the King, sent out from on high to bring the mountain into being. Coming from above, he's deeply acquainted with all that is below. And with this profound insight, he illuminates the words of the great Warrior and takes his place as our mighty mountain Guide.

THE POWER

When Jesus gave the farewell discourse, he knew that his parting instructions would be impossible for his disciples to follow without some help. But that didn't worry him because he knew that help was on the way. In fact, he knew that for the rest of time, those who sought to follow his path would have all the help they could possibly need: the help of the Holy Spirit.

"And I will ask the Father, and he will give you another advocate to help you and be with you forever— the Spirit of truth," Jesus assured his disciples as he set the stage for his departure (John 14:16-17).

"When he, the Spirit of truth, comes, he will guide you into all the truth" (John 16:13).

Jesus knew that having direct access to the Guide would be a game changer for humankind. And when he gave the mandate to remain in his love by keeping his commands, he did so knowing what kind of power would be available to those who sought to obey.

The Father, the Son, and the Holy Spirit are inseparably one. Meaning that the Holy Spirit was one of three active and indispensable participants in all of the miraculous and wonderful things that Jesus did during his time on earth. And this is a big deal because it means that when we travel with the Guide, we're accompanied by the same Spirit who enabled Jesus' ministry on Earth and by whose power Jesus was raised from the dead (Rom. 8:11).

Read that again. Let it sink in. When we travel with the Guide, we're accompanied by the same Spirit who enabled Jesus' ministry on earth and by whose power Jesus was raised from the dead!

What?!

Friends, this is our faithful mountain Guide. He's not just any old mountaineer with some fancy gear and enough experience to make a living by leading people up and down the mountain. No, he's the breath of life that awakened the mountain itself. And that's the business he has been in since the beginning: awakening. Awakening lifeless bodies into being. Awakening the hearts and minds of people to their pulse and their purpose. Awakening a world to glorify its King.

IN STEP WITH THE SPIRIT

The Guide is not a figment of our imagination. He's one with both King and Prince, and he enables us to climb toward our goal.

In Romans 8:14, Paul tells us that "those who are led by the Spirit of God are the children of God." In verse 17, he goes on to say that "if we are children, then we are heirs—heirs of God and co-heirs with Christ." Our submission to the Guide secures our relationship with the King and seals our inheritance in his eternal kingdom. Without the Guide, we might spend all our lives climbing the mountain, but we'll be climbing in vain toward a summit of suffering.

If we want to experience the guarantee and take hold of the goal, we must learn to follow the Guide. In his letter to the churches in Galatia, Paul referred to this kind of lifestyle as keeping "in step with the Spirit" (Gal. 5:25).

When you go for a walk with a friend, you don't just wander off and do your own thing. You keep in step with one another so that you can enjoy each other's company. Every so often, the pace will change. Perhaps your friend will slow down to take a sip of water or stop to tie their shoe.

In these moments, if you were to insist on keeping your own pace no matter what, the two of you wouldn't enjoy a particularly pleasant walk together, would you? In fact, what would eventually happen? You would end up walking alone.

Likewise, keeping in step with the Spirit means electing to walk with him and to follow his pace, rather than to set your own. When he moves, you move. When he slows, you slow. When he convicts, you confess. When he rebukes, you repent. When he offers refreshment or restoration, you receive.

When you "walk by the Spirit," Paul says, "You will not gratify the desires of the flesh. For the flesh desires what is contrary to the Spirit, and the Spirit what is contrary to the flesh" (Gal. 5:16-17).

The flesh, or the sinful human nature, and the Spirit are living contradictions of one another. They will not cohabit with each other in an individual's life. When you indulge the flesh, you aren't walking by the Spirit. When you walk by the Spirit, you won't indulge the flesh.

During his life on Earth, Jesus walked by the Spirit 100% of the time. But as sinful human beings, our natural bent is to gratify the flesh. Thankfully, Paul reminds us that we're not ensnared by this fate. We're called to live in the victory that Jesus claimed for us. When we make the choice to walk by the Spirit, we walk into the liberation we have been offered in Christ. Keeping in step with him empowers us to embrace and exercise the freedom that Jesus won on our behalf when he defeated death.

To walk by the Spirit, then, is not a thing of striving but a thing of choice. You cannot will yourself into a more spiritual life. But you can choose which path you'll take. You can either choose to follow your own intuition and intellect on the mountain, or you can choose to follow the Guide. And when you begin to stray from his path, because you will, you can choose to make constant, steady choices to get yourself back on track.

THE FRUIT OF THE SPIRIT

So far, we have determined that following the Guide enables us to keep Jesus' commands and remain in his love. But what happens when we do? What are the results and outcomes that we can expect when we intentionally walk in step with the Spirit?

In John 15:11, Jesus gives his compelling reason for laying out this directive: "I have told you this so that my joy may be in you and that your joy may be complete."

According to Jesus, there's a direct correlation between keeping his commands to remain in his love and experiencing full and complete joy. And this is noteworthy because it means that joy is not only a thing of choice but also a thing of obedience. When we choose to walk with the Guide and obediently follow his lead, we'll learn a new kind of joy that is richer and more beautiful than anything else the mountain has to offer.

Of course, we know that joy isn't the *only* result of following the Guide. In Galatians 5:22-23, Paul lists eight other fruits that also grow in our lives when we keep in step with the Spirit. In addition to joy, a Spirit-led life will produce love, peace, patience, kindness, goodness, faithfulness, gentleness, and self-control.

Now, that can seem like an overwhelming list if you're stuck in a cycle of striving. But remember, to follow the Guide is not to strive. It is to surrender.

We need not look at the fruits of the Spirit as a moral checklist or a spiritual scavenger hunt that must be systematically completed in order to solve some kind of enigmatic "fruit of the Spirit formula." Instead, we must surrender to the Holy Spirit and allow him to produce these fruits in us. We must choose in moments of temptation to turn to him and ask him to give us the strength to say no to our fleshly desires and to show us a better path.

Don't forget that the enemy and his army, though defeated, are still roaming around on the mountain trying to exact their revenge on the King. They will stop at nothing to thwart our progress toward the eternal kingdom. But when their arrows fly and their swords strike, we must remember that our Guide possesses all the weapons we need in order to fend them off.

Like the other fruits, joy is a response that the Guide can deploy to the frontlines for combat. Joy is like a police officer who is dispatched to stop a crime in its tracks, or a firefighter sent to save a vulnerable person from a burning building. It can even act as an emergency responder who arrives at the scene of an accident to pull a helpless victim from the wreckage and ensure they get the immediate care they need in order to begin the process of healing.

We all know that we show our true colors when the pressure is on and our circumstances turn ugly. But when we make a practice of walking with the Guide, moment by moment and day after day, we'll discover that the fruits of the Spirit grow in us and become more and more accessible in our times of greatest need. As these fruits ripen in our lives, they become primed and ready to be dispatched by the Holy Spirit himself to respond to the desires of our flesh. Joy is a response.

Keep in mind, however, that a dispatcher does not send the appropriate team to the scene of an emergency if no call comes in to announce the need. How do the paramedics know to come when a person has a heart attack or when there has been an accident on the side of the road? Someone calls it in.

You are that person. You have the responsibility to pick up the phone and dial 9-1-1. In the case of our Guide, it's not as if he isn't already well aware of our situation. But he won't force us to take the treatment if we don't desire it. So he asks us to call it in.

The Holy Spirit, from whom comes a constant flowing of the fruit of the Spirit, is ready and waiting on the other end of that phone call. He's the great dispatcher, always calm, cool, and collected, always knowing the appropriate response to any of the scrapes we find ourselves in. But we have to make the call because joy is more than just a response. Joy is also a responsibility.

ONWARD AND UPWARD

Trying to scale Mount Everest on your own as an amateur climber with no guide is a ludicrous thought with costly implications. Please never try it. But if you were to make the climb with all the right equipment and an experienced Sherpa guide to help carry your load and lead the way, you would vastly increase your chances of success, especially if you listened carefully with a teachable spirit and followed all of your guide's instructions at all times.

The Sherpa people of Nepal[16] have been residing in the Himalaya Mountains for generations. Over time, their bodies have adapted to high altitudes and have learned to function normally with the kind of low oxygen levels that present major problems for the rest of us. For this reason, guides and porters from the Sherpa ethnic group have become the unsung heroes of Everest.

These hard-working locals trek out ahead of climbers to set up camps, fix ladders and ropes in place, and carry the necessary items that put too much strain on the bodies of foreign mountaineers at elevation. Sherpa guides are not only expert climbers but also know the mountain unlike anyone else. To disregard or contradict their expertise in a high-risk situation on Everest would be much like signing your own death certificate.

The journey up the mountain of life is much the same. We have a Guide who can most certainly lead us up the mountain, regardless of the obstacles that might get in our way. Not only that, but our mighty mountain Guide is constantly running up ahead to set up rest camps, prepare the path, and carry the heavy loads that we cannot bear. We must learn to trust that he has skills and abilities on the mountain that infinitely outperform ours every time.

And as we take this journey with the Spirit of God, the ultimate guide, we realize that joy isn't some kind of checkpoint that we'll reach just over the next horizon. It certainly isn't something that you only achieve when you finally reach the top of the mountain, pat yourself on the back, and look out at the magnificent view.

Rather, joy is something experienced on the journey. When you rely on the Guide's strength, savvy, and support to help you scale the mountain, instead of striving in and of yourself, you begin to realize that the full and complete joy that Jesus talked about just sort of happens. It comes from the Holy Spirit within you and pours out to the world around you.

You don't have to be in the perfect setting, surrounded by perfect circumstances, to experience joy. It's possible at every step, every turn, every incline, and every challenge when you're willing to walk in step with the Spirit.

So how about we make a decision together, right here and now? Because I think it's time to concede that we cannot conquer the mountain on our own. Let's end this futile solo climb, with all of its wasted energy and superfluous suffering, and let's choose, instead, to live lives that are characterized by Spirit-enabled joy—joy that is complete. Let's choose to surrender our striving and offer obedience to the Guide who supplies us with all we need to reach the summit.

Let's decide right now that we're going to continue this journey onward and upward toward the goal, in view of the guarantee, and in submission to the Guide, knowing that when we walk with the Guide, we gain access to the gear.

QUESTIONS FOR REFLECTION

On "The Guide"

1. How challenging do you find it to remain in Jesus' love as you go about your daily life?

2. Have you been walking in step with the Spirit lately? If not, what steps might you need to take to realign your pace with his?

3. When we can observe the fruits of the Spirit growing in our lives, it's a good indicator that we're following the Guide. Which of the fruits of the spirit (love, joy, peace, patience, kindness, goodness, faithfulness, gentleness, and self-control) can you see actively at work in your life today? Which ones are lacking? Take some time to ask the Holy Spirit to bring growth in those areas of your life.

CHAPTER 5

The Gear

In 2016, after nearly a decade of touring the world in a rock and roll band and a few years in local church ministry, my husband, Ryan, decided it was time to go back to school and pursue a master's degree. Having always been an avid learner and a keen student of the Bible, he couldn't wait to dig into his first week-long class: Introduction to Biblical Interpretation.

As eager as a grade-school student on the eve of their first day back to class after the summer holidays, Ryan hopped into our van on a crisp November afternoon and began his first of many five-hour drives to seminary. Everything was going well… until one hour into that drive when Ryan realized that he hadn't packed a winter coat.

Now, November temperatures may not call for a winter coat where you come from. But in western Canada they most certainly do. Knowing that he would be walking to and from class every day, Ryan quickly felt the sting of his error. But that's not all.

When he woke up the next morning and walked to class in a borrowed coat, he realized that he had forgotten to bring yet another vital item for his first ever class on biblical interpretation… a Bible.

They probably should have failed him on the spot, right then and there. Seriously though, who shows up to a seminary-level hermeneutics class during the winter months in the middle of the

Canadian prairies with no Bible and no coat? It's nothing short of a miracle that he managed to pull through and walk away with a master's degree only a few years later!

I'm sure we've all been on a trip where we've realized partway to our destination that we forgot an important item. It's one thing when it's a toothbrush or a bathing suit or even a winter coat that can be borrowed or replaced. It's another thing entirely when that forgotten item is a passport and you're en route to the airport for an international flight.

The point is that certain events, situations, and conditions in life require specific planning and preparation ahead of time. It's true that we can't plan for everything, but even in the uncertainty of life, we can learn to expect the unexpected.

It shouldn't come as a surprise to us when we face inclement weather or unfavorable conditions on the mountain. These challenges are simply a reality that we'll always have to deal with along the journey. Our job, then, isn't to try to evade them, but to prepare ourselves to face them head on. This is why we must plan ahead and carry the appropriate gear.

PLANS AND PERILS

The problem is that packing all the right gear for this particular trek presents a difficult conundrum. How do you pack and carry all the necessary equipment for every possible terrain? How do you plan ahead when you have no idea what kind of conditions you'll encounter along the way or when you'll encounter them? And how do you come prepared to meet a mountain that's constantly shifting and changing?

The Khumbu Icefall[17] is the first major obstacle that climbers must traverse when they set out from base camp on the Nepali side of Mount Everest. Located at the top of the world's highest glacier,[18] this frozen waterfall is in constant motion, making it one of the most dangerous features to cross on Everest.

Without warning, mountaineers may encounter massive pieces of falling ice and treacherous cracks in the surface beneath them, resulting in the opening up of ominous crevasses at a moment's notice. When it comes down to it, all the gear in the world would not be enough to protect even the most experienced climbers against the dangers of the icefall.

The mountain of life is similarly shifting and moving. What looks one way today might look completely different tomorrow. The truth is, we simply cannot know exactly what tools we'll need at any given moment to prevail over this perilous and ever-changing slope.

Thankfully, our Guide is immune to all of the perils of the mountain. And not only that, but he comes equipped with all of the tools we might need as we encounter the vast variety of threats and terrains that the mountain has to offer. The question is, are we willing to listen to his instructions about which gear to employ and when?

In my own faith journey, I find myself frequently slipping back into a state of pride that says, "I've got this." Instead of taking pause to evaluate the situation and call upon the Guide for wise counsel, I choose to bulldoze through the barriers with my own set of tools and opinions on how things should be done on the mountain. The results of this approach are always messy on a personal level but are sometimes even catastrophic in their reach and impact on others.

As such, we must learn that sometimes, the best thing we can do on the mountain is to stop, step out of the way, and allow our Guide to do what he does best. When we submit to his instructions and employ the equipment he recommends at various stages of the climb, we'll be well-prepared to navigate the dangers of the mountain.

THE ESSENTIALS

But not all mountains are Everest. My friend Charlotte Olson trekked to the top of Mount Kilimanjaro, the world's tallest free-standing mountain,[19] in February 2020. When I asked Charlotte what she felt were the most essential pieces of equipment needed for a successful climb, I learned that Kilimanjaro can be summitted with minimal gear. As a "walk-up" mountain, Kilimanjaro doesn't require items like ropes, harnesses, or ice axes.[20] But that doesn't mean one should come ill-equipped or underestimate the challenges and risks of the mountain.

What I found particularly interesting about Charlotte's answer was that most of the gear she mentioned had more to do with her own well-being than with the way she interacted with the mountain. Her number one item was a CamelBak hydration pack and high protein snacks to ensure she stayed hydrated and energized for the climb. Next, she needed sunglasses to protect her eyes from the intensity of the sun at higher altitudes. Additionally, she listed good quality winter gear and an outer layer of Gore-Tex to keep her extremities covered, warm, and dry during that final push to the summit.

You can't climb a mountain if you're sick or dying. Many a mountaineer has turned back before the summit on account of frostbite, dehydration, or elevation-induced illnesses such as high-altitude pulmonary edema. But even lesser threats can disrupt your progress if you aren't looking after yourself.

Imagine how much harder it would be if you actually had an adversary on those mountains sabotaging your climb! We already know that joy is an essential implement when it comes to climbing the mountain of life. We also know that, because it's so important, Satan takes it upon himself to constantly attack our joy. If he can mess with it and cause it to fail, he knows he'll be able to infect us from the inside out with sin.

Joy, in a sense, is like a protective layer of Gore-Tex for the soul. When our joy is attacked, we suddenly become exposed and vulnerable to the elements. Without the covering of joy, it's as if our immune system shuts down and our enemy gains access to the very core of who we are as believers. In this state, we're much more easily infiltrated by viruses like anger, bitterness, depression, and fear.

In the same way that climbers must be very careful to look after themselves out there on the slopes to ensure their expedition doesn't meet an unnecessary and early end, we must prioritize our well-being on the mountain of life if we want to have any hope of reaching our goal. And if we understand that joy is fundamentally connected to protecting our core, then we'll be all the more diligent about employing equipment that both generates and maintains joy on the mountain.

This book isn't meant to be an encyclopedia of all the equipment that enables joy on the mountain of life. In essence, that book already exists, and it's far superior to mine. It's the same book that Ryan forgot to bring with him on his first day of seminary, and it alone is the true manifesto for the joy revolution we're after.

All the same, even though I cannot catalogue all of the tools we can benefit from on the mountain, I do want to take the time to point out three key pieces of practical gear that prove extremely useful when it comes to cultivating intentional, biblical joy.

1. **GRATITUDE**

Another piece of equipment that Charlotte couldn't do without on her Kilimanjaro expedition was a good pair of trekking poles. Walking up a mountain would be one thing if the path to the top was completely smooth. But this is rarely the case.

For Charlotte, poles were essential on Kilimanjaro because they helped keep her balanced and secure along the journey. Gratitude is just such a tool on the mountain of life. When the terrain beneath our feet is rocky and unstable, gratitude gives us the extra support we need to steady ourselves and carry on with the climb.

The book of Exodus chronicles the story of Israel's deliverance from slavery in Egypt. After generations of suffering at the hands of their oppressors, it was time for God to fulfill his promise to liberate them from bondage and bring them into a fruitful land that they could call their own.

Forty years and nearly three books of the Bible later, we come to Deuteronomy 26. In this chapter, God laid out a detailed instruction guide for how the Israelites were to respond upon finally entering and taking possession of the promised land.

Commanding them to take some of the first fruits of their harvest and bring them to the altar of the Lord as an offering, God was inviting his people into the practice of gratitude. In order to keep themselves balanced and in tune with him as they began their new lives in this distant land, they were to first reflect upon and remember how he had delivered them and their families from oppression in Egypt.

And God wasn't exactly subtle with his instructions. In Deuteronomy 26:11 he said, "Then you and the Levites and the foreigners residing among you shall rejoice in all the good things the Lord your God has given to you and your household."

Did you catch that? *You shall rejoice.* I can't help but be left with the distinct impression that joy isn't exactly optional for those who seek to follow God. In fact, God commands it. Like the Israelites, we too have been delivered from great oppression. Therefore, we too must be intentional to set aside time to express gratitude and to worship joyfully.

But when God answers a prayer or something great happens in our lives, how easy is it to just say a quick "thank you" and then move on? To be completely honest, a lot of times, I don't even remember to do that. I just glaze past it without a second thought, finding myself in the company of the nine ungrateful lepers who failed to return to Jesus to express their gratitude after he healed them from their debilitating disease (Luke 17:11-19).

We must remember that gratitude, like joy, is a responsibility. It's something we must actively work at and consciously pursue in order to keep ourselves grounded as we climb the mountain. It makes me wonder if, perhaps, God set up some of these offering systems in the Old Testament to train the Israelites in thanksgiving. By making it their responsibility to offer back to him some of the good things he had given them, and inviting them to do so in a spirit of worship and joy, he taught them to demonstrate the discipline of gratitude.

Though we're no longer bound by the specifics of the ceremonial laws of the old covenant, the lesson remains for us today: we are to practice gratitude. We are to regularly reflect on and remember who God is and what he has done for us.

And the thing is, no matter how difficult our circumstances may be at any given moment, we can always be grateful for salvation. The Israelites were delivered from physical oppression in Egypt. We've been delivered from spiritual oppression on the mountain of life. And when we choose to reflect on the goodness of this gift and express gratitude even in the midst of hard times, it enables joy and propels us up the mountain.

Has God given you and your household good things? Then give thanks and rejoice!

Okay, I know what you're thinking. To simply "give thanks and rejoice" is easier said than done. And you're not wrong. It's true that actively choosing gratitude and joy can sometimes feel like an impossible task. When it does, it's imperative that we check our focus.

2. **FOCUS**

Snow blindness is a condition that occurs when the ultraviolet rays of the sun reflect off the snow and literally sunburn a person's eyeballs, causing them a temporary loss of vision that can last up to forty-eight hours.[21] Sounds comfortable, right?

Climbers at high altitudes must remember that the power of the sun is heightened at elevation, and, therefore, must keep their eyes protected if they don't want to end up blind and incapacitated. With a good set of snow goggles, they'll be able to keep their eyes fixed on the goal without the distraction of pain and discomfort. As we navigate the mountain of life, our focus acts as a pair of protective goggles, ensuring that we don't become blinded by distractions and stray off the prescribed path.

The book of Nehemiah recounts the restoration of the walls of Jerusalem after God's people returned to their motherland from exile in Babylon. Now, if the word exile sounds kind of harsh and extreme to you... that's because it is. We don't have much context for it nowadays, but in this case, it meant that the Babylonian empire had invaded the nation of Judah, captured their men, women, and children, and carried them off to live in a foreign place under the oppression of a tyrannical ruler.

In the time of Nehemiah, however, the people had been allowed to return to their capital and rebuild the city. After the city wall was completed, the nation gathered together and Ezra the priest stood before them to read the Book of the Law, which is to say, the parts of the Bible that had already been written at this point in history. Suddenly enlightened to the wrath of God toward their sin, the people grieved the hopelessness of their wretched state. But Nehemiah, a self-appointed lay leader to the people, wouldn't have it. Instead, he told them to get up, wipe their faces, and get on with the party.

"Go and enjoy choice food and sweet drinks, and send some to those who have nothing prepared. This day is holy to our Lord. Do not grieve, for the joy of the Lord is your strength" (Neh. 8:10).

Nehemiah was concerned about the people's focus. He recognized that they were more focused on their circumstances than they were on

God. But this was a day set apart for the Lord, a day for celebration, not one for sorrow and sadness. He knew that indulging in excessive grief would only turn their attention away from God and put it on themselves and their shortcomings. Wallowing in their guilt wasn't going to change anything; and besides, this wasn't the time or the place. They were here for a party, to marvel at what God had done.

Don't get me wrong; it's important to understand the weight and severity of our sin. We are to humbly and contritely confess our sins to God. But when we let our sins, or anything else for that matter, take our focus off him and his goodness, we risk spiritual snow blindness and miss out on the joy of the Lord.

In a sense, we can choose to see every day of our lives as a day set apart for God. We are his, and he has given us so many blessings that we can celebrate every single day. But in order to do that, we must take our eyes off ourselves and focus them on the Lord who is our source of joy and strength.

God illustrated this principle to me one evening as I was sitting alone at my kitchen table, spending some time in prayer. On the wall directly across from me was a large window. As I sat there in quiet communion with God, a soft impression came over my heart that prompted me to get up out of my seat and wander over to this window. Sitting down on a stool in front of it, I did my best to tune in to that little voice inside saying, "Look out the window. What do you see?"

It was a dark, winter evening and I had bright lights on in the house, turning the window into more of an enormous mirror. Naturally, the very first thing I saw was my own reflection quite clearly. But I quickly noted that if I changed my gaze, I was able to see outside into the dark night.

The light from my window illuminated the nearest neighbor's fence and the trees along their fence line. But if I looked even harder, I could see beyond the trees and into the backyard, though barely, since everything was so black. Finally, as I focused harder still, I was surprised to find that through the space between the houses, I could see all the way across to the other side of the cul-de-sac, where my eyes caught sight of a tiny red light shining in the distance.

As I focused on that little red beam, I realized that my reflection in the window had effectively disappeared. In fact, the further away I focused my gaze, the less I found that my own likeness in the window was blocking my view.

But as I fixed my eyes on nearer objects, my reflection became correspondingly visible. Sometimes, I could see it only slightly, while, at other times, it was more prominent. But one thing remained consistent: when I truly focused my eyes on that distant light, I forgot about seeing my reflection altogether.

God spoke to me in that moment and left me with this impression on my heart: "Your reflection disappears when you focus on the right place."

It hit me like a ton of bricks. I realized that over time I had become snow blind. I had taken off the goggles of focus and turned my gaze away from the goal and onto the damaging reflection of myself. So many of my actions and choices in life, though seemingly good, were often being influenced more by my own aspirations, plans, and perfectionism than by the will of God.

All too often on the mountain of life, the enemy attacks our joy by misdirecting our focus. Whether it's our sins, our ambitions, our problems, our relationships, our busy schedules, or even our leisure activities, if it removes our goggles and reduces our ability to focus on the Guide as he leads us up the mountain, it can create lasting damage and quickly steal our joy.

When that happens, we end up hyper-focused on ourselves, running around in circles without an end in mind, forgetting entirely about the goal and what it takes to get there. But when we turn our gaze heavenward and fix it on the glory and goodness of our King, his joy becomes our strength and his love becomes our mission.

3. <u>MISSION</u>

Mountaineers who climb on snow-covered, icy peaks all require a crucial piece of safety equipment known as crampons. Crampons are essentially ice cleats that attach to your boots and provide necessary traction and grip on dangerous, wintery surfaces. You won't get very far in the heights of the mountains without appropriate footwear. Even a leisurely mountain hike requires a good pair of hiking boots.

The same is true on the mountain of life. We must ensure our feet are aptly fitted to tackle the mountain. Ephesians 6:15 suggests that it's our missional readiness, which "comes from the gospel of peace," that ultimately equips our feet to climb this mountain.

What is this "gospel of peace"? The gospel is the central message of the entire Bible. It's the good news that although our sin creates enmity between us and God, he chooses to extend an offering of peace and grace that eclipses the fatal effects of our sin. The fact that we've been offered total forgiveness through Jesus' selfless sacrifice on the cross is the most beautiful news known to man.

In John 3 we read a conversation that took place by the cover of night between Jesus and a distinguished Pharisee named Nicodemus. During this conversation, Jesus uttered the famous words of John 3:16: "For God so loved the world that he gave his one and only Son, that whoever believes in him shall not perish but have eternal life."

Our mighty Prince of Peace incarnated on the mountain to carry out a divine mission of love. Surely, he was there to defeat the darkness, but not because the scheming enemy posed some kind of grave threat to the safety and stability of the King himself. The imposing threat, rather, was that of eternal separation between the King and his people.

In his great love, the King could not allow such an impossible chasm to come between himself and the people he loved. By sending his Son, the King illuminated his mission to seek and save the lost—the very mission that we're invited to participate in as we traverse the great mountain.

It's important to understand that the purpose of this mission is not to produce joy in our lives. Truly, we're to participate in the mission of the King because the great Warrior Prince commissioned us to do so before he went to prepare a place for us in the eternal kingdom. In light of the great victory he has won on our behalf, it's only fitting that we should respond to the Prince by taking up his mission and carrying it out under the direction of our Guide. Nonetheless, what we find when we do so is that joy abounds in the missional life.

The apostle Paul always made this principle crystal clear when he wrote letters to the churches that he established throughout the course of his ministry. To see his disciples serving God and living out the gospel was a continual source of joy in his life.

Consider the pure and poignant way he described it in 1 Thessalonians 2:19-20. He wrote, "For what is our hope, our joy, or the crown in which we will glory in the presence of our Lord Jesus when he comes? Is it not you? Indeed, you are our glory and joy."

Paul understood that the only thing he could take from this life into the next was the people that he impacted with the truth of the gospel. He was already looking forward to the crown of righteousness which would be awarded to him when he reached the end of his days, but here we see just what would make that crown shine in all its glory. It would be covered with inscriptions; engraved with the names of all those whose lives had been touched by him and whose journeys to the summit he'd taken part in motivating.

When we fit our feet with the gospel of peace and choose to live missionally, we unlock a secret joy that won't come from anything else on the mountain. And not only that, but we get to participate in spreading the beauty of the gospel to a world in need.

"How beautiful on the mountains

are the feet of those who bring good news,
who proclaim peace,
who bring good tidings,
who proclaim salvation..." (Isa. 52:7a)

Does this mean we must live our lives as a carbon copy of the apostle Paul's? No. And we must not kill ourselves trying.

Paul himself taught that we have all been given different gifts, which we should actively use according to our own measure of faith (Rom. 12:6). We must each embrace our unique gifts and realize that, no matter what they are, they all exist to advance the gospel. And when we function in our God-given giftings for the purpose of expanding his kingdom, we gain access to a wellspring of joy unlike any other.

TIME TO CLIMB

I promised you earlier that this wouldn't be an encyclopedia on all of the gear required to climb the mountain of life, and I intend to make good on that promise. I would love to discuss ice axes, helmets, and ropes, but that would be a book all on its own. Instead, I encourage you to study the encyclopedia itself, to set out on a quest to discover the deep truths of the mountain by acquainting yourself well with the words of its Maker.

In doing so, know that the endless wealth of useful riggings and devices that are housed in the storeroom of the great King are available to us at all times on the mountain through our liaison, the Guide. Be ready to receive from him both the instrument and the instruction to use it because, more often than not, it will feel counter to your nature to comply.

In that sense, I would urge you to ask yourself, right now, if you're willing to trust the Guide's wisdom and discretion as he provides you with the gear you'll need to scale the mountain of life. Trust is never easy. It takes unrelenting courage and discipline, neither of which come naturally on the mountain. But consider the journey we've taken so far. We have fixed our eyes on the goal and embraced the guarantee. We have learned to follow the Guide and to make use of his gear.

The only thing that remains for us now is to climb. The question is, do you have the guts?

QUESTIONS FOR REFLECTION

On "The Gear"

1. How does gratitude balance you on the mountain journey? If you've lost your balance recently, what might you do to recover it?

2. When was the last time you suffered from spiritual snow blindness? What did you do to readjust your focus? (Or, perhaps, what do you need to do to readjust your focus right now?)

3. What is the gospel? Are you actively engaged in God's mission to proclaim the gospel message to the world?

CHAPTER 6

The Guts

In *The Voyage of the Dawn Treader*, author C.S. Lewis tells the daring tale of siblings Lucy and Edmond, along with their cousin Eustace, who are whisked out of our world and into the land of Narnia. The children team up with King Caspian and his crew in a swashbuckling adventure to sail the seas in search of the eastern edge of the Narnian world.

Along the way, this merry company explores a host of unique islands, one of which, by the way, became the inspiration for my daughter Avra's first name. But neither this particular fictional island nor my sweet little girl is the reason I mention the fifth installment in the *Chronicles of Narnia* series. Rather, I bring it up because I want to talk about Dark Island.

Dark Island, as it turns out, wasn't so much an island as it was more of a deep, sinister darkness that loomed on the horizon. According to Lewis, the only way to imagine such a place would be to picture yourself "looking into the mouth of a railway tunnel—a tunnel either so long or so twisty that you cannot see the light at the far end."[22]

As they sailed into this mysterious darkness, the travelers suddenly began to hear screams of agony and terror coming from somewhere inside of that impossible gloom. Crying for mercy, a crazed man was brought aboard their vessel, begging them with all urgency to turn about and retreat.

Having been tortured by the trickery of the darkness for too long, this stranger now revealed the secret of Dark Island: it was the place where dreams come true. But not daydreams or the happy dreams that you don't wish to wake up from. No, at Dark Island, all of your worst and most terrifying nightmares would become a reality. As you recall the sinister images that have woken you in the night, the magic of the island brings them to life before your very eyes, leaving you immobilized by fear and unable to escape.

Fear has the same sort of effect on the mountain of life. Whether rational or irrational, it can be completely debilitating. I spent ten summers working at a Bible camp just north of Lloydminster. One year, there was a lot of talk about a snake that lived close to one of the cabins in the woods. Do you have any phobias? I have a few. But the most severe of them all is, and always has been, snakes.

Now, a person who wasn't immobilized by fear would have rationally considered that this wasn't the first snake that had ever resided within the camp boundaries. A person who wasn't immobilized by fear would have also recognized that going into the woods on any given day wouldn't guarantee a meeting with this particular snake. A person who wasn't immobilized by fear would have appreciated the fact that even if they were to encounter the snake in the woods, it would only be a harmless garter snake that would be more afraid of them than they were of it. And a person who wasn't immobilized by fear would have evaluated their track record of having come across exactly zero snakes in the wild during their several years on staff at this camp and realized that the chances of meeting one were really quite low.

But I was a person immobilized by fear.

So, what did I do? I avoided the woods all summer long. When the whole camp gathered to play Capture the Flag or Mission Impossible in the bushes, I would slip off to the office and bury myself in paperwork. I became so obsessed with my fear of running into this snake that I could no longer carry out some of the regular functions of a camp leader.

I never did encounter the snake that summer. But looking back, I think I may have encountered something worse. Instead of enjoying my summer in the great outdoors, as I had done for so many years previous, I spent it trapped on Dark Island, terrorized by my own imaginations.

Hopefully the fears that you encounter on the mountain of life aren't quite as irrational and over-the-top as some of mine. But the point is that fear is real and, if we're not careful, it can make an awful mess of our lives. If we want to conquer the mountain of life and one day arrive at our goal, we cannot allow ourselves to become imprisoned on Dark Island.

AFRAID, YET FILLED WITH JOY

Fear is a joy thief. Few things along the mountain journey are quite as effective at stealing our joy as fear itself. While we know this to be true, our crafty enemy twists the truth to make us buy into the myth that we cannot experience fear and joy at the same time.

And so, over time, we become conditioned to believe that fear is in control and always wins. We give our joy permission to run for the hills anytime fear rears its ugly head. Tragically, we succumb to the black haze of Dark Island.

In Matthew 28:1-8, we read the story of two women whose lives were transformed by a radical joy that couldn't be shaken by fear. These two women were Mary Magdalene and, in Matthew's own words, "the other Mary."

Can we just stop here for a minute and acknowledge the fact that this woman was forever immortalized in the Bible as "the other

Mary"? Can you imagine if, for the rest of history, you were only ever referred to as "the other Brian" or "the other Michelle"? Thankfully, I have a weird name, so I've never had that problem. Never in my life, to my knowledge, have I been referred to as "the other Talasi." Thanks, Mom!

But I digress. According to Matthew, these two women discovered the empty tomb on the morning that Jesus rose from the dead. This story is recorded in the Bible by Matthew, Mark, Luke, and John, all focused on different details. As such, some elements of the story are unclear, including who was present at the tomb that morning. But nuances aside, let's take a look at Matthew's unique perspective on this event.

For starters, in verse 2, Matthew describes a violent earthquake that took place as an angel appeared to roll the stone away from the entrance to the tomb. The guards on duty passed out from fear, terrified by the angel's appearance, but the women were given special instructions by this heavenly messenger.

"Do not be afraid," the angel told them. "For I know that you are looking for Jesus, who was crucified. He is not here; he has risen, just as he said. Come and see the place where he lay. Then go quickly and tell his disciples: 'He has risen from the dead and is going ahead of you into Galilee. There you will see him'" (Matt. 28:5-7).

As the women rushed off to tell the other disciples about this bewildering encounter, Matthew 28:8 says that they were "afraid yet filled with joy." On the one hand, this was a terrifying experience. We can't quite gather from the text whether or not the women were present when the earthquake happened, but I imagine that it wasn't a miraculously isolated event, which occurred only within a small perimeter of the tomb. Don't quote me on this, but I think it's much more plausible that a violent earthquake of that magnitude was so widespread that, wherever the women were at the time, they would have felt it.

We also don't know from the text whether or not these women actually saw the angel descending, or if they had any interactions with the guards before they passed out. Both Luke's and John's accounts suggest that the place was entirely abandoned with the stone already rolled away when the women arrived. But whatever the case, Matthew is clear about the fact that these women experienced two emotions simultaneously. Fear and joy.

Any of the above events that *could* have happened would have been enough to elicit fear. But even if the women didn't feel the earthquake, didn't have an unnerving interaction with the guards, and didn't see an angelic being descending from the heavens, Matthew informs us that the experience shook them. They were afraid. I mean, they did encounter an angel whose "appearance was like lightning" (Matt. 28:3). That alone would leave me stranded on Dark Island!

But at the same time, these women couldn't have received better news. Jesus was alive! Though they may not have been able to fully process what this meant yet, they were overjoyed. Somehow, their fear and joy managed to mingle in this extraordinary moment as they departed from the tomb and began to make their way back to their friends.

JOY THAT ECLIPSES FEAR

Here's the thing I love about this. Fear could have stopped them, but joy motivated them. They were afraid, *yet filled* with joy. They were full of apprehension, but it didn't slow them down. They ran to do what they knew they needed to do: tell others the good news that Jesus was alive!

I love this story because it tells me that fear and joy can coexist. I've always seen these two emotions as diametrically opposed to one another. I genuinely believed that for joy to truly be present, fear would have to be eradicated. This is another reason why, for many years, I didn't even bother with the pursuit of joy. I believed it would be futile because I knew that my overwhelming fear would always win.

But that's not the story we read in Matthew 28:1-8.

These women were terrified, yes. But they were also elated. Their respected teacher and beloved friend, the Messiah, whom they thought was dead, was now living and breathing! And not only that, but they were starting to connect the dots and realize that Jesus had indeed predicted all of this. Did you catch what the angel said in verse 6? "He is not here, he has risen, *just as he said*" (Matt. 28:6, emphasis added).

Luke's account of this incident says it like this:

"He isn't here! He is risen from the dead! Remember what he told you back in Galilee, that the Son of Man must be betrayed into the hands of sinful men and be crucified, and that he would rise again on the third day. Then they remembered his words" (Luke 24:6-8).

The fact that the women remembered this might seem like an insignificant detail on the surface, but it really matters. Because as they remembered what Jesus had said to them, this outrageous claim that he would die and come back to life, the pieces of the puzzle started coming together to reveal the fulfillment of all God's promises.

Jesus' prediction that he would be raised from the dead came true. This was the culmination of everything he had claimed about himself and taught while he was with them. All of those wonderful truths and promises were real and proven in this moment. Jesus is alive, and he's the Son of God!

This is a short and simple story, but it's powerful because it shows us that fear doesn't always have to win over joy. The circumstances these women found themselves in leading up to verse 8 weren't joyful. Jesus had died. There had been a violent earthquake. The tomb was empty. A person who looked like lightning was saying crazy things to them. These circumstances alone could really mess a person up.

But even before they ran into Jesus in the flesh, it was joy, rather than crippling fear, that drove their response to the situation. They had the courage to remember what Jesus said, and to believe it could really be happening.

This kind of joy can characterize our lives as well. We weren't present in that moment. We weren't there when the earthquake happened or when the stone was rolled away. We didn't see the empty tomb.

But the tomb is still empty today.

Jesus, who died for your sins and for mine, is alive. He has conquered the mountain and defeated the darkness on our behalf. Do you know what that means? It means that the *same joy* the women felt at the empty tomb is available for you and me too: courageous joy that eclipses all fear.

COURAGEOUS JOY

Courage is recognizing that fear is real yet choosing to press on anyway. In the greatest act of courage known to man, our mighty Warrior Prince confronted the darkness that cloaked the mountain and conquered it for good. But it wasn't the battle itself that made this act courageous. It was the fact that the Warrior had to face fear.

On the night before he died, Jesus felt deeply distressed and told his disciples, "My soul is overwhelmed with sorrow to the point of death" (Matt. 26:38). While it has been debated among scholars whether or not Jesus actually felt fear, I have a hard time separating the torment and anguish he experienced in those moments from feelings of trepidation.

Jesus knew what was coming. He knew what he was about to endure. He asked God more than once for this cup of suffering to be taken away from him. Furthermore, we know from Hebrews 4:15

that Jesus can fully empathize with our human experience because he was tempted in every way that we are.

No matter which side of the argument you land on as to whether or not Jesus *felt* fear, at a minimum, we can know that he *faced* fear. He was tempted with fear. And what's the temptation to fear if not, at the very least, a momentary surge of apprehension that entices you to give in to despair?

Jesus didn't give in to his despair. And Hebrews 4:15 also offers a very important qualifier about Jesus' humanity: he was without sin. But he wasn't without temptation. He wasn't without a very personal, very human knowledge of the emotional experience of fear. Yet he chose to press on anyway. Fear couldn't hold our mighty Warrior because he radically trusted the King and the Guide to make good on their part of the plan.

Courage requires trust. Even in the story of the women at the tomb, we see that their trust in Jesus enabled their courageous joy. They believed—they had faith—that this news wasn't too good to be true. Indeed, their initial response would have been very different if they hadn't believed the angel.

They could have been cynical or angry, thinking it was some kind of cosmic practical joke. They could have been too busy wallowing in their sorrow to look up and notice the resurrected Jesus standing there in their midst, which we can read about if we continue on to Matthew 28:9-10. Instead, they chose to trust, and it filled them with courageous joy.

BUT I TRUST

Joy and trust are inextricably connected. When you choose joy, particularly in the midst of difficult circumstances, you choose to trust in God. And when you trust God on this deep, personal level, it produces more joy in your life. Then, in true cyclical fashion, as joy is discovered by trusting God, it compels you to trust him even more. And I'm sure you can guess what happens next! Naturally, you discover more joy, and the cycle continues.

We see this demonstrated in the life of David, whose story we can find in the Old Testament. From a common shepherd boy to a revered king of Israel, David was a man who lived through the highest of highs and the lowest of lows. He led mighty armies into victory with great cunning and savvy, but he also spent a huge portion of his life on the run, trying not to be killed by some of the people closest to him.

And, for someone who had a special relationship with God and was arguably the most celebrated king in the history of Israel, David was by no means perfect. He made plenty of mistakes. Beyond that, he suffered a great deal of inner turmoil. Many people believe that David struggled with depression, which is important to note as we learn from his life.

In Psalm 13, David poured out his emotions onto paper as he struggled through an excruciating inner battle. He felt utterly alone and forgotten by God. Exhausted by his tumultuous thoughts and burdened by the constant outward reality that death and destruction awaited him at every turn, David experienced unrelenting sorrow in his heart during this devastating season of his life.

David spent the first four verses of this six-verse lament pouring over his anguish. Dealing with intrusive thoughts, feelings of abandonment, and very little motivation to carry on—all struggles that I deeply identify with—David pleaded with God for answers and affirmation.

In verse 3 he said, "Look on me and answer, Lord my God. Give light to my eyes, or I will sleep in death." Poor David just wanted to feel like God noticed him. After feeling so deserted and demoralized, a simple acknowledgement of his existence would have been enough to keep him going. Otherwise, he confessed, he was ready to just give up and die.

But then, all of a sudden, something happens in the Psalm that gets me every time. Verse 5 begins with three small words that change everything.

"But I trust…"

Come again, David? Would you like to rephrase that part? You're depressed. Your thoughts are tormenting you. You're being hunted and defeated by your enemies. You feel utterly abandoned by God. And your response to all of this in Psalm 13:5 is, "But I trust in your unfailing love; my heart rejoices in your salvation"? What am I missing here?

David actually did this consistently in his Psalms, which I appreciate because it means that this wasn't a one-time thing for him. This active choice to pursue courageous joy through trust in God is something that David regularly practiced when he was feeling down in the dumps and overcome by fear and anguish.

David modeled that joy is a spiritual discipline. To be clear, he did not *feel* joy in this moment. But somehow, in the midst of his brokenness and pain, he still *chose* joy. He spoke it. He resolved in his heart to believe it. He made a disciplined decision to both want and pursue it.

David's example proves that it's possible to choose joy, even in the face of great suffering and fear. The more we know and trust about God's character, the easier it is to rejoice.

THORNS AND THISTLES

But what if you're in the thick of it right now? What if somewhere along the mountain path you fell behind, lost sight of the Guide, and started doing your own thing? What do you do now that you find yourself face-to-face with a rock wall that you don't have the gear or the guts to climb, or tangled up in a dense thicket of thorns that you cannot break free from on your own? How do you choose trust when doubt and worry are closing in on you from every side?

We all have times of doubt. We all have times when our worries scream louder than the truth. And just like fear, worry is a master when it comes to stealing our joy.

I mean, what does worry do, after all? In the parable of the sower (Matt. 13:1-23), Jesus demonstrates how worry and the stresses of this life choke out the word of God, making us unfruitful. He refers to this kind of worried, choked-out life as seeds sown among thorns. This person can be a follower of Jesus, they just don't produce fruit because the thorns and thistles keep choking out the word of God and stealing their joy.

The mountain of life is covered in thornbushes. They were planted there by the enemy as a scheme to trip us up and immobilize us, much like Dark Island. But as always, the King has a solution.

Isaiah 55:12-13 says:

"You will go out in joy
    and be led forth in peace;
the mountains and hills
    will burst into song before you,
and all the trees of the field
    will clap their hands.
Instead of the thornbush will grow the juniper,
    and instead of briers the myrtle will grow.
This will be for the Lord's renown,
    for an everlasting sign,
    that will endure forever."

These words were first written for God's people as a beautiful promise that he would deliver them from captivity in Babylon. We talked a little bit about their liberation and return to their homeland in Chapter 5, so we know that God made good on his promises in that case!

But ultimately, this promise points forward, far beyond this national deliverance from earthly exile. It speaks to the deliverance that would one day come for all of humankind through Jesus Christ. In fact, the deliverance of the Hebrew people from their Babylonian captors would become a picture and a display of the promise itself and would point to the coming eternal deliverance from enslavement to sin.

And all of creation would experience the joy of this coming salvation. Not only would humankind go forth in joy and peace as a result of this gift, but the mountains and the trees, creation itself, would join in the chorus of praise to the Lord. Healthy, fruitful foliage would begin to come up where previously there were only thorns and thistles. And just as this was a promise for God's people that their land would be made healthy and fruitful again, so it is a promise for us, that the King is not finished with us. He will not abandon us on the mountain.

We may come to Christ covered in thorns and thistles, overcome and overwhelmed by fear, but surely, he can make us new. He can brush away the brier and create space in us for a fresh start, for new life.

COMFORTABLE CAPTIVITY

But so often on the mountain, we let the thorns and thistles win. We get ourselves so good and stuck that the thought of breaking free terrifies us even more than the thought of remaining trapped. Though our wise and gentle Guide offers to clear away these thorns, we cling to them and fear their removal because we know how they'll scratch and wound us as they're jostled and stirred up in our lives. We fear pain in the moment, so we give in to the thorns and relinquish the long-term freedom and fruitfulness that the Guide offers.

Then we wonder why this promise from Isaiah 55 doesn't seem to be for us. We find ourselves thinking things like, *God said that I would go out in joy and be led forth in peace, but all I feel is fear and worry!*

I've struggled with this conflict for most of my Christian life. Why? Because I refused to let go of the thorns and thistles. I refused to let go of perfectionism, striving for my own righteousness, and the fears and worries that would keep me up at night. Instead of letting Jesus clear away the briers to make way for juniper and myrtle tress, I chose to remain among the thistles—the worries and pressures of worldly life. I've lived in this soil so often. There is no joy there.

When it comes to clearing away the thistles, every one of us is left with a choice. The Israelites actually had to choose to leave Babylon. They weren't swept up in a supernatural cloud and whisked back to Jerusalem. They had to pack up all their belongings and leave the lives they knew. Of course, it seems only natural that they would have wanted to return to their motherland. But let's not overlook the possibility that captivity might have become comfortable for some of them.

Now, I realize that the thought of experiencing comfort within the confines of oppression sounds ridiculous, but don't we do this all the time? We become so accustomed to the chains the enemy uses to keep us enslaved that, eventually, they become a strange sort of safety net for us.

I've often said that living with mental illness feels like a life sentence in jail. You become a prisoner of your own mind and you slowly lose your ability to function in the outside world. All you know is the four walls of your prison cell. Anything outside of captivity becomes foreign, distant, confusing, and even more worrisome than the stress of being incarcerated.

This experience has never been more real to me than during the seven years of my life when I was enslaved by an eating disorder. Sure, overcoming it meant being set free from my bondage, but it also meant having to face a world of terrifying unknowns.

It's possible that some of the captives who were granted permission to return to Jerusalem might have felt something similar. Like all of us, they had a choice to make. They could keep their chains and remain enslaved or follow God into the wide-open world of freedom.

It seems like a no-brainer, but it becomes a little more complicated when you consider that with freedom comes risk, vulnerability, and uncertainty. Exile might have been awful, but at least it was what they knew. Who knows what kind of dangers would await them out there in the great, big world? All the same, the promise was connected to their choice. And there would be no reclaiming of their homeland for the people who chose to stay behind for fear of the unknown.

Likewise, we have to choose whether or not we'll accept the clearing of the thorns and thistles from our hearts and allow the Holy Spirit to make us fruitful and new. Yes, the process will sting a little. It might even sting a lot. But we must not allow our present pain to hold us back from future freedom.

COURAGE, DEAR HEART

Remember, courage is recognizing that fear is real yet choosing to press on anyway. If we want to make it up the mountain, we must cultivate courage every day by embracing the reality that fear and joy can coexist, trusting in God even when life gets messy, and choosing to allow our Guide to clear away the thorns so that we can walk in joyous freedom.

It's interesting to note that the seafarers aboard the Dawn Treader were also sent a guide to lead them out of the darkness.

Barely squeaking out a whisper of a prayer to the son of the Emperor-beyond-the-Sea, Lucy called upon Aslan, the great lion, to send help. And sure enough, help came in the form of an albatross, illuminated by a beam of light from above. As it circled the boat, Lucy alone heard it whisper in her ear, "Courage, dear heart."

Our Guide comes sweetly in the name of freedom, whispering the same message to those who are willing to hear it. "Courage, dear heart."

The mountain path isn't easy. The journey is long, and it takes a lot of guts.

But you'll know it was worth it when you start to see juniper and myrtle trees springing up in your life. I'm not a botanist, so I don't know much about those particular species of trees, but they sound awesome. And I do know that sometimes all it takes is a little bit of healthy growth to boost morale and keep us moving on the mountain.

We all need that now and again. Because we're in it for the long haul, and it takes more than just guts to play the long game. If we want to stay the course and persevere to the end, we're also going to need a healthy dose of grit.

QUESTIONS FOR REFLECTION

On "The Guts"

1. Courage is recognizing that fear is real yet choosing to press on anyway. Where in your life do you need the most courage right now?

2. What is your initial reaction to the joy-trust connection discussed in the section titled "But I Trust"? Can you observe a correlation between how much you trust God and the level of joy you have in your life?

3. What "thornbushes" are you caught up in right now? Are you ready to choose freedom? What would that look like for you?

CHAPTER 7

The Grit

In 2007, my husband, Ryan, and his bandmates learned that you can't believe everything you see in the movies.

Cruising down I-70 under the moonlit sky, Kiros was en route from their last show in Maryland to their next gig somewhere in the Midwest. Roadies and band members were sprawled out all over the 15-passenger van that served as their tour bus in those days. Trying to catch a wink of sleep as they observed their strict regimen of traveling at night and disc golfing during the day, Ryan found himself riding shotgun on this particular occasion, dressed in typical night-driving attire: his underwear.

Suddenly, a few miles before reaching the infamous interchange between I-70 and the Pennsylvania Turnpike in Breezewood, PA, the driver detected something alarming. No one remembers what caught his attention first. Was it the sight, or the smell? Either way, it was undeniably smoke.

While the rest of the crew slept soundly in the back, the driver pulled over on the side of the interstate and Ryan hopped out of the front seat to assess the situation. He didn't need to look under the van to observe the smoke seeping out from beneath it, but he bent over anyway to see if he could locate the source of the problem.

"Fire!" he shouted in a panic as he took off sprinting down the highway, wearing nothing but his boxer briefs. He was no fool. He had seen plenty of action movies. And if there was anything he knew about a vehicle on fire, it was that it could only be moments away from a deadly explosion.

Cowering in the distance, he watched in disbelief as his groggy bandmates piled out of the van and, instead of running for safety, began collecting valuables—including his own. What were they thinking? Every moment they spent in close proximity to that van was one step closer to certain death.

But the van never did blow up, sending his buddies flying 30 feet through the air in every direction. Take every installment of *The Fast and the Furious* that you have ever seen and throw it out the window, because that's not how it went down on the side of I-70 in the middle of the night. After a while, the flames fizzled out and the boys called a tow truck to come drag them and their broken-down tour van to the nearest mechanic in Breezewood.

For the members of Kiros, the rock-and-roll life wasn't exactly all glamour and goldmines. After spending nearly a decade on the road, they had been through three vans, two buses, and three cargo trailers, averaging 60,000 plus miles per year. You can only imagine the repair bills that come in when you're logging that kind of time on the road.

In fact, the part of the story I haven't told you yet is that less than 24 hours before flames interrupted their I-70 night drive, this same van had been in a shop in Maryland having the transmission repaired. Evidently, that repair was an epic fail.

They never did retrieve that van from the mechanics in Breezewood. They cut their losses, cleaned it out, and abandoned it forever. But, as you know, this wasn't the end of their transportation troubles.

Their next van died in Washington, after which they borrowed a pickup truck to carry six of them through their next few dates in Canada and back down to Kentucky where they bought their first bus. That bus died when Tyler drove it under a low railway bridge in Calgary, and their next bus had to be retired because of a bad engine that was draining their bank account.

With fortune like this, you might wonder how the boys of Kiros managed to carry on for all those years. What kept them going when times were tough? What inspired them to push forward when all the odds were stacked against them?

Put simply, they had grit.

PASSION AND PERSEVERANCE

Angela Duckworth, author of *Grit: The Power of Passion and Perseverance*, defines grit as "passion and perseverance for long-term goals."[23] As a Christian rock-and-roll band, Kiros was motivated by the core belief that their mission to share the hope of Jesus with as many people as possible outweighed their circumstances every time.

Killing time at a truck stop for a few days in a strange, little town in Pennsylvania certainly tempted the guys to pack up, call it quits, and head home. But at the end of the day, they had a goal in mind and were willing to do whatever it took to see it fulfilled. They booked many of their own shows, hustled hard to sell albums and merchandise, and marketed like pros in a time before YouTube sensations and modern social media. When challenges came, they found ways to creatively overcome them.

For example, breaking down in Breezewood created an opportunity to increase pre-sales for their up-and-coming record, *A Single Strand*. Reaching out to fans to support their "van fund," they started selling autographed copies of their soon-to-be-released album at a higher price point. As a result, they sold more records, reached more people, and bolstered their dream.

According to Jon Acuff, "A dream you don't have to fight for isn't a dream—it's a nap."[24] The Kiros boys weren't out there napping on the road. Okay, to be fair, most of them probably did nap daily to make up for all the headbanging, late nights at Denny's, and long days on the disc golf course. But they weren't napping when it came to their dreams. In that sense, they epitomized grit.

If grit is passion and perseverance for long-term goals, then where is it more needed than on the mountain of life? Of all the long-term goals we might strive for on the mountain, the ultimate goal of making it home to receive our crown is, by far, the longest. Unreachable until the end of our earthly lives, we cannot expect to take hold of it without exhibiting some grit along the journey.

But how? Where does grit come from? How do we get it?

There's no use in me rewriting Angela Duckworth's bestselling book. She's more of an expert on the subject than I'll ever be. But what I can do is take a look at the Bible's interpretation of grit and what it looks like to pursue it from a biblical perspective, beginning in the book of James.

FELICITATION

James 1:2-3 says, "Consider it pure joy, my brothers and sisters, whenever you face trials of many kinds, because you know that the testing of your faith produces perseverance."

According to Barnes' *Notes on the Bible*, to consider it pure joy when you face trials means to "regard it as a thing to rejoice in; a matter which should afford you happiness. You are not to consider it as a punishment, a curse, or a calamity, but as a fit subject of felicitation."[25]

If you feel like you must now immediately rush off to look up the definition of felicitation, don't worry. I've got you covered. A quick search on Dictionary.com will tell you that felicitation is "an expression of good wishes; congratulation."

In other words, James is saying that we should give ourselves a great big pat on the back when we face hardships in life. We should literally congratulate ourselves. Why? Because it's the opportunity to face hardships with joy that ultimately produces the grit we need to reach our heavenly goal.

The trials you go through as a Christian aren't going to inherently elicit feelings of joy. Joy will most likely never be your instinctive, natural response, at least, not initially. Joy, in these circumstances, is a responsibility. It's something that you'll have to choose and actively pursue with a certain degree of grittiness because, if you don't, the trials and sorrow will overtake you.

Negative emotions infect a joyful heart. But to consider it *pure* joy would be to see every part of the trials you face as an opportunity for growth. James is clearly not suggesting that we should give joy a fleeting thought or a half-hearted effort when we face hardships as Christians, as I personally so often do. Instead, he urges us to go all-in on joy because when we do, we block potential infections from the outset and prohibit them from entering at all.

LIFE LESSONS

A few years ago, Ryan and I went through a challenging season in which several false and hurtful accusations were made against him and his involvement in our camp ministry. Though we knew these accusations would be impossible to prove because of their blatantly fictitious nature, we were still devastated by the circumstances we found ourselves in.

Looking back, it's almost as if I can see my spirit separate itself from my body and watch from the sidelines as my response to those circumstances slowly began to infect my broken, unprotected heart. Like a cancer spreading through my cells, all of the negative emotions I felt in that situation—bitterness, anger, fear, uncertainty, betrayal, worry, and hopelessness—infiltrated my heart and released poisonous toxins into the very core of my being.

Within months, I was on the brink of a nervous breakdown. I've never experienced more anxiety in my life than I did during that ordeal. I was a broken, angry, and hurting woman. As I reflect on that season now, having eventually come out the other side stronger and more in tune with God, I can see how my unhealthy response to those circumstances led me astray.

For starters, I stopped following the Guide. In fact, I stopped climbing altogether. I completely shut down and binged out on Netflix for a few days. Instead of clinging to hope and embracing joy, knowing that God was in control and that he was my vindication, I chose to wallow in my misfortune.

And I don't throw around the word "chose" lightly. I *know* I chose. As I said earlier, it was as if I stepped out of my own body and watched myself choose fear over trust, bitterness over forgiveness, and despair over joy. I knew it was wrong. I knew I was headed down a perilous path. But I did it anyway and suffered the consequences of an infected heart.

Thankfully, our God is endlessly gracious and kind. He brought me through that season and healed my heart through repentance, forgiveness, and vulnerability. But I learned a valuable lesson. I learned that when it comes to James 1:2-3, I cannot let my guard down for a second. This kind of joy is a constant and crucial responsibility that I can't afford to ignore.

Fast forward three and a half years. Once again, Ryan and I have found ourselves in another painful ministry situation that we cannot control. Try as we may to fight for what we believe is healthy and true, many times we've felt as though we keep coming up against insurmountable walls with our hands tied.

But I learned my lesson the last time. So now, as we face these troublesome moments in ministry, I've chosen to anchor my hope to the unchanging promises of God rather than the fickle nature of our circumstances. I have elected to choose joy and trust in the midst of an arcane and agonizing situation in order to protect my heart, grow in grittiness, and continue moving up the mountain.

STEADFASTNESS

According to James 1:2-3, the stories I've just described to you can be seen as tests of faith. Verse 3 posits that the testing of our faith develops perseverance, or some translations say "steadfastness." And what happens when our faith is tested? We are given an opportunity to display trust in God.

In Chapter 6, we discussed that to choose trust in God is to choose joy. When you boil it all the way down, joy is trust. And it's the choosing of joy/trust in the midst of our suffering that produces steadfastness in us.

Steadfastness has to do with unwavering resolution. It's a fancier, more Bible-y word for grit. And yes, I just used the word "Bible-y"—because I'm the author of this book and I get to make calls like that (and my editor approves)!

The fact is that there are times on the mountain when it all comes down to steadfastness. At times, we've more or less done everything right: we've walked faithfully with the Guide, utilized all the right gear, and exhibited a whole lot of guts, but we still come up against impossible obstacles.

Storms roll in, the terrain torments us, our gear starts to fail, and it feels almost like the Guide has abandoned us. We know the instructions he last gave, but every moment in this madness makes it harder and harder to remember them.

In times like these, you simply have to make a choice. Will you follow? Will you obey? Will you resolve to trust that the Guide is good and that you can have faith in his directions, even when you can't see him? Even when it seems you are at an impasse?

When you do, steadfastness is at work. And we want steadfastness to do its work in us because something awesome happens when it does. Check out James 1:4: "Let perseverance (steadfastness) finish its work so that you may be mature and complete, not lacking anything."

The idea is that, as steadfastness continues to grow and work in us, we'll ultimately be brought to a place of completion. And where do we reach completion? On the summit. Without steadfastness, we cannot reach the end of our earthly lives, the pinnacle of our mountain journey, with our faith intact.

A WORTHY LIFE

It seems like it's getting easier and easier to walk away from the faith all the time. With access to a world of infinite information and endless entertainment at our fingertips, we can amuse ourselves with all kinds of distractions and fill our brains with useless knowledge at the drop of a hat. Steeped in this culture, so many climbers lose sight of the goal. They allow their faith to waiver and be manipulated by the world, turning their hope into a weak or false gospel.

But when we allow steadfastness to work in us, it enables us to cling to God's truth and grow in our knowledge of him so that we can reach the summit with a stronger faith than we had when we started this journey. In his letter to the church at Colossae, Paul prayed that God would allow the believers there to do just that: to be filled "with the knowledge of [God's] will through all the wisdom and understanding that the Spirit gives" (Col. 1:9).

Paul didn't want the Colossian Christians to taper off in their faith. Instead, he wanted them to "live a life worthy of the Lord and please him in every way" (Col. 1:10). But what does that mean? How do you know if you're living a life worthy of the Lord?

Paul answered this question in Colossians 1:10-12. He said that you'll know you're living this kind of life when you are "bearing fruit in every good work, growing in the knowledge of God, being strengthened with all power according to his glorious might so that you may have great endurance and patience, and giving joyful thanks to the Father, who has qualified you to share in the inheritance of his holy people in the kingdom of light."

Interestingly enough, various translations of the Bible differ slightly on their use of the word "joy" in this passage. As we just read, the New International Version talks about "giving joyful thanks" in verse 12. But if you were to read the English Standard Version, you would find it renders these words as "endurance and patience with joy" in verse 11, leaving just "giving thanks" in verse 12.

At first glance, I find this somewhat confusing. In one case, joy is tied to the act of giving thanks, while in the other case, joy is connected to endurance and patiently persevering. So, which one is it? How can we know if we're getting it right?

I've realized that maybe this doesn't need to be so confusing after all. Maybe the idea is that joy should permeate everything in our lives, from thanksgiving to endurance, from the stuff we're grateful for to the stuff that's hard. Whenever we give thanks, we should do it joyfully because joy is a response to the wonderful goodness of God. But whenever we have to patiently endure difficult circumstances, we should also do that joyfully because joy is a responsibility for believers who want to "live a life worthy of the Lord" (Col. 1:10).

A WORD ON CIRCUMSTANCES

You'll notice that the word "circumstances" has come up a lot in this book (thirty-five times so far, to be exact, but who's counting?), and there's good reason for that. In Chapter 2, I told you that if we go through life allowing joy to be a response to our circumstances, we will largely forfeit our ability to experience any joy at all. Because here's the thing: to require favorable circumstances as a prerequisite for joy is really no different than perfectionism.

Perfectionism is another one of those bottled lies sold by the shady merchant on the side of the mountain path. Masquerading as virtue and righteousness, perfectionism says that there's no place for joy in an imperfect life. But the problem is that the perfect life simply doesn't exist, at least, not on the mountain. If we wait for everything in our lives to align perfectly before we give joy a chance, we'll find ourselves waiting forever.

That's where grit comes in. Grit is okay with imperfection. Grit sees that life is a mess and chooses joy anyway.

And this grittiness, this joyful endurance, keeps us focused on the goal, the guarantee, and the Guide, no matter what comes at us on the mountain. It's what allows us to experience the kind of inexpressible joy we read about in 1 Peter 1:8, instead of the inexpressible sorrow that proliferates from a focus on our circumstances.

I'm no stranger to inexpressible sorrow. My guess is that you've been there too. And I'm convinced that part of the reason our society is drowning in sorrow these days is that we're obsessed with our circumstances and how much better our lives could be. We become so fixated on measuring up or achieving more, when we should be celebrating the fact that because we *can't* measure up, Jesus has achieved *everything* we'll ever need.

A WORD ON WEAKNESSES

Don't get me wrong. I'm not trying to reduce the global mental health crisis down to a single, oversimplified solution. I recognize that we can't just say "stop focusing on your circumstances" and expect the world to wake up happy again tomorrow morning. I've lived with mental illness for most of my life and I, of all people, understand how much more complicated it is than that. All the same, I am suggesting that perhaps it's time to redefine some of our values as a culture.

For example, why are we so afraid of our weaknesses? Our culture values strength and confidence, but so often that requires us to put on a face and pretend like we have it all together when, really, we feel like we're struggling to keep our heads above water. I think this is why we're trending more and more toward transparency as a culture all the time. Millennials are tired of having to fake it. Gen Z-ers actually just don't buy it. Yet our culture still resists this shift toward vulnerability and transparency.

But something powerful happens when we accept our weaknesses and limitations for what they are and allow the power of God to work in spite of them. Paul demonstrates this principle in 2 Corinthians 12:7-10 when he talks about the thorn in his flesh, an ailment of some kind that tormented him regularly. Paul doesn't go into detail about this "thorn," so we don't know if it was physical, mental, or some other external factor, but we do know that Paul found it to be a major burden as he went about his life and ministry.

I think we all have some of these nagging struggles in our lives that we just can't seem to get rid of. I've felt this way about depression and anxiety many times over the years. I've crumbled under the weight of it, thinking I'd be so much more effective and successful in my calling if God would just take the problem away.

Perhaps you've felt this way too. Paul certainly did. In fact, he pleaded with the Lord several times to remove this burden from his life. But he didn't receive the response any of us would hope for. "My grace is sufficient for you," Jesus told him. "For my power is made perfect in weakness" (2 Cor. 12:9).

In other words, Jesus chose not to heal him, at least, not for the time being. We don't know if the thorn was ever removed later in his life, but we do know why it was there in the first place: to keep Paul humble and to help him rely on God's strength rather than his own (2 Cor. 12:7,9).

And it worked! In 2 Corinthians 12:9-10, Paul goes on to say, "Therefore I will boast all the more gladly about my weaknesses, so that Christ's power may rest on me. That is why, for Christ's sake, I delight in weaknesses, in insults, in hardships, in persecutions, in difficulties. For when I am weak, then I am strong."

When I read these words, I'm reminded that there is a unique beauty in my struggles and weaknesses because they give me an opportunity to put the power and the glory of God on display in my life. When God gives me the courage, the strength, and the grit, to get up day after day and fight the inner battles in my soul and to combat those lies that seek to control my mind, it demonstrates the healing power of God. It shows that even in my weakness, in my sinful, broken, and messed up state, Christ's power can rest on me.

In Chapter 6, we learned that it's entirely possible to be set free from the thornbushes that get us all tangled up on the mountain. But even then, sometimes, we'll still walk away from that obstacle with a thorn stuck in our side. And *sometimes,* those thorns remain in our flesh in order to point us and others to the King.

Paul's example teaches us that we can choose joy even with a thorn in our side. Like Paul did, we can delight in our hardships and struggles, knowing that we grow in grit when we do so. We can boast with gladness about our weaknesses, because our weaknesses highlight the mighty strength of God at work in our lives. And that is liberating.

PERSONAL DISCLAIMER

My guess is that you've been through your fair share of hard times in life. If you're reading this book right now, there's probably a decent chance that you struggle with joy. In fact, I would even venture to say that many of you can readily point to a thorn in your life right now.

If that's you, I want you to know something. I understand how painful Scripture can be sometimes. I know what it feels like to have well-meaning people quote upsettingly specific Bible verses to you, with no real regard for your feelings or the ins and outs of your daily struggle. I have felt the weight of the truth come down on me like a hammer when it has been delivered in an insensitive, untimely manner.

Here's one that might feel like salt in the wound when you're in a dark place: "Rejoice in the Lord always, I will say it again, rejoice" (Phil. 4:4).

Another one might be: "Do not be anxious about anything, but in every situation, by prayer and petition, with thanksgiving, present your requests to God. And the peace of God, which transcends all understanding, will guard your hearts and your minds in Christ Jesus" (Phil. 4:6-7).

I have been vexed by both of these verses on multiple occasions. When I'm in a tough spot, they don't give me hope at all. In fact, in those cases, it feels like all they do is shine a light on my failure.

Now, please don't misunderstand me; these verses are found in Scripture. They are the word of God, meaning that they are fundamentally important and flawlessly true. We have a responsibility as believers to obey these instructions.

But let me tell you what doesn't *feel* encouraging when you're at the bottom of a depressive low or in the middle of a panic attack: a Bible verse that effectively says, "Just stop feeling anxious, then you'll get to experience the peace of God." I mean, really? Come on. If someone tells me that verse in the middle of a panic attack, my primary thoughts are, "Well, I can't do that right now. So I guess I'm doomed."

Again, we have a responsibility to obediently follow God's instructions because they're a part of his big story. But we also need to remember that they aren't the whole story. We need to look at the entirety of Scripture to gain a more complete understanding of the individual instructions found therein. When we do that, we can come to appreciate that Philippians 4 is describing a lifestyle that happens when we follow the Guide, not an emergency response prescription for a panic attack.

My prayer is that none of the words written in this book will come across as a flippant quoting of Scripture to people who are hurting. I recognize that some of the ideas I'm presenting may be hard to swallow at times, but I pray that you won't walk away from here feeling like I've laid out an impossible standard that you'll never measure up to.

Because it's really not about measuring up. It's not about perfection, right? I've learned that when it comes to my darkest moments, I need to remember the part of the story where God looks at me, calls me by name, and says, "Talasi, my grace is sufficient for you. My power is made perfect in weakness. This weakness, this battle, this struggle that you're facing right now is an opportunity for you to put my power on display and find out just how strong and gritty I'll make you in the midst of it."

I find hope in that. And I pray that you will find hope in that. If you've ever found yourself between a rock and a hard place on the mountain, wondering if God has forgotten about you or why he's taking his sweet time in addressing this burdensome thorn in your side, I want to encourage you today to remember that even in this darkness, God's grace is sufficient for you. His power is made perfect in your weakness. In these moments real grit truly shines because when you are weak, then you are strong.

GOING FOR GLORY

There's no question that we'll have to endure suffering on the mountain. And there's nothing like a long, arduous climb to bring out our weaknesses in full force. But the beauty of it all is that we're climbing toward the promise of a better future. Every day, as we give joyful thanks and joyfully endure the hardships of the mountain, we take one step closer to that great and glorious goal.

This is what I would call living with an "eternity mindset." To live with an eternity mindset means choosing to rejoice in present pain because of the glory of future freedom. Jesus did exactly that during his time on Earth, and he invites us to do the same. He invites us to rejoice in the opportunity to share in his sufferings because it means that we'll also one day share in his glory.

In Romans 8:18, Paul says, "I consider that our present sufferings are not worth comparing with the glory that will be revealed in us."

Are you ready to embrace this attitude? Yes, climbing the mountain is wearisome and harrowing at times, but the goal is eternally worth it. So, let's bring all the passion and perseverance we can muster as we push toward the summit. We're in this together and we're not looking back. We've got our eyes on the prize and we're going for glory.

QUESTIONS FOR REFLECTION

On "The Grit"

1. How would your life be different if you were to consistently look at the trials you face as opportunities to develop grit?

2. Have you ever experienced the toxic results of negative emotions spreading like a poison throughout your heart and soul? What will you do differently next time to avoid such a damaging outcome?

3. What does it mean to you to "live a life worthy of the Lord" (Col. 1:10)? Are you living such a life?

CHAPTER 8

The Glory

In 2002, Her Majesty Queen Elizabeth II, along with her husband Prince Philip, Duke of Edinburgh, visited my home province of Manitoba during her Golden Jubilee tour.

Born and raised in Canada, I never knew a time before Queen Elizabeth's likeness appeared on one side of all my coins. As a child in elementary school, growing up in a constitutional monarchy simply meant singing "God Save the Queen" in addition to the national anthem at the start of each school day (and only in my very early years before the practice was abandoned). As I grew older, my knowledge of the Commonwealth and our place in it was limited to Canadian history lessons and the occasional movie that depicted the monarchy.

The 2002 Golden Jubilee tour, however, sparked my interest when I learned that my choir would be singing for the Queen during her visit to Winnipeg in October of that year. Though I knew very little about Queen Elizabeth, I was awestruck at the thought of performing in front of one of the most famous and powerful women in the world.

Sadly, my memories of that moment have faded with time. Aside from my vivid recollection of the frigid cold we felt down on the waterfront that day as we waited for Her Majesty to arrive, the rest of the details remain distant and vague.

Nonetheless, I know that an elaborate event of this magnitude required a great deal of planning and preparation. My choir was just one of many acts that would perform together to create a grand display of Manitoba culture to delight Her Majesty, and we alone had our fair share of rehearsals leading up to the royal visit.

When royalty takes the time to visit their subjects, their presence is received with a great welcome and fanfare. Copious time, effort, and energy are expended to prepare a celebration fit for a king, one that appropriately venerates their glory and honor.

Psalm 149:2-3 says, "Let Israel rejoice in their Maker; let the people of Zion be glad in their King. Let them praise his name with dancing and make music to him with timbrel and harp." For me, these verses evoke the memory of those unique moments at the meeting of the Assiniboine and Red Rivers in Winnipeg, where I got to perform for the Queen of England all those years ago.

Psalm 149 paints a similar picture of a stately display of music, art, and praise, all poured out from a people who deeply desire to honor their sovereign. These words may have been originally addressed to the nation of ancient Israel, but the message rings true for us today: joyful praise is core to our DNA as God's people.

On the mountain of life, we are daily invited to participate in a magnificent procession of praise which celebrates the resplendence of the King. As his subjects, we have a great privilege and responsibility to rejoice in his goodness and majesty. When we celebrate the blameless character and mighty works of our God with joyful praise, we bring our hearts, souls, and spirits into alignment with one another in a grand display of reverence for the glory and honor of our King.

A PERSONAL KING

But If I'm being honest, singing "God Save the Queen" as a little girl in grade school is a much different kind of memory for me. Far from a joy or honor, it was no more than a simple obligation that I carried out at the expectation of my educators.

After all, who was this queen? What had she done that I could tangibly see? I didn't know her personally, nor did I understand the relevance of her existence in my day-to-day, six-year-old life. And no matter how devoted, compassionate, and respected this queen may have been, the reality was that the vast majority of her subjects would still never meet her in person. There would always be a certain degree of separation between her and her people.

It's different with the King of the mountain, though. We needn't look very far to see a tangible example of his powerful goodness at work in our lives. Just look at the planet that we call home, with all of its plants, animals, lands, and oceans. From the tiniest insect to the loftiest heights of Mount Everest, God made it all. And if the good leaders of our world are worth celebrating, how much more so should we bring praise, glory, and honor to the One who formed the world?

But there's more. God also formed humankind. He gave us brains and sanctioned us to become thoughtful beings who could design, create, and invent just like him! He developed science and art, philosophy and psychology, all of the valuable tools that help us understand the world and each other. God has *made* amazing things.

And God has also *done* amazing things. At the cost of great personal sacrifice, he has invited us all to experience a personal relationship with him. Not wanting to turn us into puppets or force us to love and serve him against our will, he gave us the ability to make our own choices.

But with free choice comes the opportunity to rebel. And throughout history, the human race, the crown of God's creation, has consistently exercised our capacity to rebel against our Maker, forging a great chasm of separation between the people and their King.

But this Sovereign wouldn't stand for such a separation. Even from the creation of the world, God put a plan into motion to redeem what was lost and make everything new. At the opportune time, he sent his Son, Jesus, to earth to take the punishment for our sins upon himself so that we could be forgiven for our rebellion, reckoned righteous, and restored to right relationship with him!

In this kingdom, we *all* have equal opportunity to engage personally with our Monarch and to celebrate his glory. The evidence of his work is all around us at all times. "For since the creation of the world God's invisible qualities—his eternal power and divine nature—have been clearly seen, being understood from what has been made, so that people are without excuse" (Rom. 1:20).

To subscribe to the prevailing ideologies of our day, which present God as impersonal, irrelevant, or unnecessary, is to ignore the evidence that's staring us in the face. God is sovereign and he's good. We are the creation, and he is our Creator. Everything we are comes from him. What right do we have to be ungrateful for anything?

When you consider the fact that your life is created, designed, and originated by God, suddenly you realize that you don't lay claim to any of it at all. Meaning that joy in our Maker is not only the appropriate response to who he is and what he has done; it is also the responsibility of a person who is truly grateful.

It's impossible to measure the inestimable depth and value of all that God has done for us. But one thing is for sure: joy is the right response to the work of God's hands because it expresses our gratitude and celebrates his glory, which is the sum total of all he is, all he has made, and all he has done.

A DISPLAY OF BEAUTY

Years ago, while studying with YWAM, I heard it said that to speak of God's glory is just another way to describe his beauty. John Piper puts it like this: "The glory of God is the infinite beauty and greatness of his manifold perfections."[26] In other words, the immaculate goodness and holiness of God is what makes him so deeply beautiful. And this beauty, which is put on display in the world around us, is the mark of his never-ending glory.

The mountain itself is full of God's beauty. We can see it in the tall, towering trees, in the rich, rushing waterfalls, and in the stunning skies above. "The heavens declare the glory of God," Psalm 19:1 reminds us. "The skies proclaim the work of his hands." We need only to keep our eyes open as we navigate the mountain path, and we'll catch constant, unmistakable glimpses of God's magnificent glory.

We can also see it in ourselves and in one another. Every one of us on the mountain was created to display God's beauty. We were made in his image to reflect the exquisite likeness of our King. And we do that inherently, without even thinking about it or realizing it, because the mark of our Creator is woven into the core of our being. All that's unique and wonderful about each one of us points to the creative genius of our Maker.

But we can also display his beauty in the way that we live, specifically when we align ourselves with Jesus and allow his Spirit to dwell within us. Jesus is, after all, "the radiance of God's glory" (Heb. 1:3). When we take the time to get to know him and choose to model our lives after his, that radiance flows through us as well. To walk in step with the Guide along the mountain path, abiding in his love, resting in his truth, and following his directions, is to demonstrate the glory of the King through our submission and joy.

Furthermore, Colossians 1:27 tells us that "Christ in us" gives us the "hope of glory." The very essence of hope is that it points to the future; it's an expectant desire for things that have not yet come to pass. Having the "hope of glory" is powerful because it means that not only do we display the glory of God through our presence and actions right now on the mountain, but our lives also become instruments that point to an even greater revelation of his glory that is still yet to come.

Joy is a response to the glory of God, both present and future. When we grasp this truth, we realize that there's no need to get caught up in the struggles and the challenges of this journey we call life. There will always be suffering on the mountain, but we can joyfully "participate in the sufferings of Christ, so that [we] may be overjoyed when his glory is revealed" (1 Pet. 4:13).

Accordingly, we're called to "set [our] minds on things above, not on earthly things" (Col. 3:2). We must actively choose not to allow the day-to-day distractions of the mountain to take our minds off the goal and the guarantee.

Now, I don't mean to minimize the difficulty of this task because it's never easy to keep our focus in the right place. It requires a great degree of self-sacrifice, a willingness to die to yourself and embrace the life of Jesus. But when you do so, Colossians 3:3-4 says that "your life is now hidden with Christ in God. When Christ, who is your life, appears, then you also will appear with him in glory."

A ROYAL WEDDING

Glory. What a grand and magnificent day that will be for those who have chosen to set their allegiance to the King. A flash of light and a thunderous roar will draw their eyes toward the summit where they will see him, the great and mighty Warrior Prince, coming down the mountain with all the power, authority, and splendor of the King, calling the allegiant to himself.

It's time.

Time to end the suffering. Time to snuff out that meddling enemy once and for all. Time to put all things to right on the mountain. And best of all, it's time for a wedding!

You see, our Warrior did more than just defeat the darkness when he conquered the mountain, as if that alone wasn't enough. He also made a promise to his beloved, sealing forever his commitment to one day return for her, to bring her home to be his bride.

This is the final glory that we look forward to: the royal wedding, a grandiose spectacle, unlike anything you've ever seen. Throughout the Bible, this matrimonial metaphor is used to describe the relationship between Jesus and the church, which is to say, the people who have surrendered their will to his and have chosen to make him the Lord of their lives.

Unwaveringly committed to his future bride, Jesus suffered the worst fate imaginable in order to rescue his betrothed from the claws of her captor and "to present her to himself as a radiant church, without stain or wrinkle or any other blemish, but holy and blameless" (Eph. 5:27). The apostle John, whose divinely inspired vision gave us the book of Revelation, describes the bride of Christ as "the Holy City, the New Jerusalem." Brilliantly shining and covered in precious stones (Rev. 21:2,10-11), she would not be shining with her own brilliance, to be sure, but glowing with the permeating radiance of God.

And it wasn't just New Testament authors who employed this metaphor. Hundreds of years before John's revelation, Isaiah prophesied that this New Jerusalem, which represents true reconciliation between God and his people, would no longer be seen as deserted or desolate, but be known as "Hephzibah," meaning "my delight is in her," and "Beulah," meaning "married" (Isa. 62:4).

This is a picture of redemption. It's the story of a woman whose life has been ravaged by guilt and pain. She has prostituted herself to be used and tossed out by men, and she has been left to navigate the harsh realities of life, forsaken and alone.

Yet in Isaiah 62:5, we read that "as a bridegroom rejoices over his bride, so will God rejoice over [her]." Despite the wretchedness of her past, she will be loved as though none of it has ever happened. She will be delighted in, as a young man delights in the wife of his youth.

For centuries, the people of God habitually rebelled against him, dividing their loyalties and turning away to worship false gods. As I read through the Old Testament, I'm often left feeling like God had every right to abandon his people, a people who were bound and determined to live life on their own terms, regardless of the cost. But God didn't forsake them. Nor does he forsake us.

Just as God redeemed his people from exile in Babylon, so too would he redeem his church from the chains of sin. And when he restored the people of Judah to their own land, allowing them to return to Jerusalem and rebuild their home, he pointed forward to the final glory when all things would be rebuilt and made new, in honor of the royal wedding.

PREPARATION

Dreams have a certain way of demonstrating timeless truths in the most ridiculous and nonsensical ways imaginable. One night, for example, I dreamt that I was to appear in a friend's wedding as one of her bridesmaids. Naturally, it was my job to attend to the bride, to help her get dressed and ready for the big day, and to jump at her beck and call if she ever needed anything. Except, on the day of the wedding, I was nowhere to be found.

In true dreamlike fashion, I kept finding myself in all the wrong places and wondering why on earth I wasn't where I needed to be when I needed to be there. Constantly getting caught up in this delay or that distraction, I didn't come through for the bride once. I completely shirked all of my wedding responsibilities and took the title of worst bridesmaid ever.

As frustratingly painful as this dream was, I couldn't help but draw a parallel to our role as Christians. Those who follow Jesus are called to attend to the bride of Christ, yet it doesn't take much to distract us from this calling. So often, we get caught up in trivial concerns, busying ourselves with pursuits that have very little bearing on eternity.

But as attendants, we must honor our responsibilities to the bride. And if this metaphorical bride refers to the complete body of believers, then we belong to this body too. Therefore, our charge to make her ready for the great wedding is twofold.

1. __PREPARE OURSELVES__

First, we must make ourselves ready. In Matthew 25:1-13, Jesus tells the Parable of the Ten Bridesmaids. Awaiting the arrival of the groom so that they could join his procession and attend the wedding feast, five of the bridesmaids came prepared, while five did not. When the groom took a long time coming, the bridesmaids fell asleep, waking up only moments before his arrival. Those who had come prepared had enough oil in their lamps to reach the feast, but the others came up short. Having to leave at this critical moment to go and purchase more oil meant that these unprepared bridesmaids missed out on the procession and arrived at the feast too late to enter.

As we journey along the mountain path, we too must make every effort to prepare ourselves for the final glory. "When Jesus returns to take his people to heaven, we must be ready. Spiritual preparation cannot be bought or borrowed at the last minute."[27]

We alone are responsible for our own spiritual state of affairs. It's up to us to discover what spiritual preparation looks like through an honest examination of God's word. How can we prepare if we haven't taken time to accurately understand the instructions we were left with?

Take 1 Thessalonians 5:16-18, for example: "Rejoice always, pray continually, give thanks in all circumstances; for this is God's will for you in Christ Jesus." Here we can see three simple acts that fall squarely within the will of God and offer practical help as we make ourselves ready for the return of Jesus. Yet, if you're anything like me, you ignore these instructions daily.

You don't rejoice always, because life is complicated. It's full of sadness and fear, and to continually choose joy regardless of your circumstances takes more effort than you're generally willing to expend.

You forget to pray continually, because your brain is already overloaded with the ridiculous amount of information you expect it to contain at any given moment. Besides, you're too busy overanalyzing every detail in your mind... When could you possibly find the time to pray?

Then there's giving thanks in all circumstances. You believe that gratitude is powerful, but you just can't bring yourself to apply it unconditionally. Because sometimes, in the midst of deepest sorrow, gratitude feels almost like a knife to the throat; it's sharp, it's violating, and you get the vibe that you'll probably bleed to death if you let it anywhere near you.

But we cannot ignore our responsibility to make ourselves ready for Christ's return. To rejoice always, pray continually, and give thanks in all circumstances are instructions that, by nature, take time to complete. It will be too late to "rejoice always" when we see the Warrior Prince come riding down the mountain in search of his bride because "always" encompasses all of the moments that came before that one. So if we want to be ready, we must begin now.

2. <u>PREPARE THE CHURCH</u>

Secondly, we must make the church ready. Certainly, God delights in each of us as individuals, but we as individuals are not the bride. The beauty of this great wedding is that the whole of the church, the community of all those who have placed their faith in God across the span of the ages, will be united together as one and then bonded to Christ as his bride for all of eternity.

Therefore, as members of this beautifully diverse body, we must be fundamentally committed to the global church. We must "make every effort to keep the unity of the Spirit through the bond of peace" (Eph. 4:3). We must each use our unique gifts "to equip his people for works of service, so that the body of Christ may be built up until we all reach unity in the faith" (Eph. 4:12-13a). We must radically love people who are different from us. We must obey the great commission to "go and make disciples of all nations" (Matt. 28:19), reaching the unreached people at the ends of the earth and in our own neighborhoods. And we must live out the prayer that Jesus taught us to pray, that God's will be done, and his kingdom come, on earth as it is in heaven (Matt. 6:10).

It's true that the final glory is coming, and that joy, in its purest form, will be ours in that moment. But when Jesus taught us to pray "your kingdom come, your will be done, on earth as it is in heaven," he was not inviting us to idly wait until we enter the eternal kingdom to experience the radical joy and glory of God. He was inviting us to faithfully endeavor to have God's kingdom come into our midst today—to manifest all the joy and the glory of the Lord on the mountain path right now.

Our call to make the church ready as a bride-in-waiting is not a call to complacency, to casually wait for the engagement period to end. Rather, it's a call to embrace the reality that we are living in the moment of preparation every single day.

This is not some kind of vague, long-term arrangement with no real plan for a future wedding. To God, "a day is like a thousand years, and a thousand years are like a day" (2 Pet. 3:8). To us it might seem like a long time coming. But in the scope of eternity, this wedding is imminent, and we're not living in an ambiguous engagement period. So, we should not be ambiguous in our preparations. As the church, we should overtly and actively participate in doing God's will now, as it is always done in heaven.

If, in heaven, the throne room of God will be overflowing with a great multitude of people from every nation, tribe, and language (Rev. 7:9), then we must seek to prepare a diverse bride right now. If, in heaven, we'll all live in perfect unity with one another regardless of the disagreements we had on earth, then we must strive to reconcile conflicts within relationships right now. And if in heaven we'll experience ultimate joy in the presence of our God, then we must practice the presence of God through intentional joy right now.

We must make ready the bride of Christ. When we do, we dress and adorn her in fine linen and precious gems, accenting the true, intrinsic beauty of who she is and all the reasons why Jesus loved her so deeply in the first place. We participate in the promise of God to complete the good work that he has begun in each and every one of us. And we prepare ourselves and one another for the greatest joy we'll ever know: that moment when we enter into God's glory.

IMAGINE

What should it be like to enter God's glory? We cannot truly know. The royal wedding is a metaphor, a means by which we can deepen our understanding of things beyond our comprehension, as have been many of the devices in this book. But the true revelation of glory is coming. "For now we see only a reflection as in a mirror; then we shall see face to face. Now [we] know in part; then [we] shall know fully" (1 Cor. 13:12).

Until then, we can only imagine.

We can imagine that moment when our feet reach the summit, and everything changes in a flash. It's that moment when you see the King coming toward you with a crown in his hands, shiny and glistening in the light of his glory. "Well done, good and faithful servant!" he testifies with both the pride of a father and the pomp of a king.

After delicately placing that golden diadem upon your head, he takes you by the hand and leads you along a smooth, golden path until you're standing before the majestic doors of a grand, towering cathedral, more exquisite than the most famed pieces of architecture you recall from the world below. Ascending the steps, your heart flutters as those great and mighty doors begin to open, revealing the throne room of the King.

And there, seated in his rightful place on the throne in grace and majesty, is the mighty Warrior. The King of your heart and the Deliverer of your soul. The one who ascended the mountain to win your freedom and make all of this possible.

How can you enter his presence? You have nothing to offer and your clothes are but rags from the rigors of the climb. Or are they? You look down now to find that you're dressed in fresh, formal garments, fit for nobility. And even this, you realize, is a gracious gift of the King, who has chosen to clothe you in the righteousness of his Son. This same righteousness crowns the Warrior's own head and clothes the multitude of undeserving nobles who, like yourself, have gathered to pay homage to their Rescuer.

It was because of his profound victory on the mountain that "God exalted him to the highest place and gave him the name that is above every name, that at the name of Jesus every knee should bow in heaven and on earth and under the earth, and every tongue acknowledge that Jesus Christ is Lord, to the glory of God the Father" (Phil. 2:9-11). And this is precisely the sight you see before you now upon the glassy floors of the great throne room: every knee bent, every head bowed low, and every crown cast down at the feet of the One who conquered death.

To behold his glory is to see his beauty, a blinding beauty that tells the story of a single life lost to save the lives of many. You find yourself now among the company of the worshippers, flat on your face in unspeakable awe, offering up the only thing you have to give, your crown, which was always his in the first place.

""Hallelujah!" you cry in unison with the others. "For our Lord God Almighty reigns. Let us rejoice and be glad and give him glory! For the wedding of the Lamb has come, and his bride has made herself ready. Fine linen, bright and clean, was given her to wear" (Rev. 19:6b-8).

This is the moment you've waited for all your life; the pinnacle of your existence. Inexpressible joy! A light, floating kind of joy that's free from all the burdens of the mountain but is still somehow so much richer and deeper for having experienced them down below. It's a joy that will never fade—a joy that, in fact, *cannot* fade, for the King has closed the door on sadness and suffering forever.

Your mountain journey has come to an end, but somehow you know this is just the beginning. There will be no more toiling, or torment, or trials, or tears... only life and joy. For the One who ascended the mountain with your name written on his heart has brought you here to live with him in the eternal kingdom—forever.

You are finally home.

Joy.

Everlasting joy.

QUESTIONS FOR REFLECTION

On "The Glory"

1. How central is "joyful praise" to your Christian walk? What could you do to make it more of a priority?

2. Are you actively engaged in your calling as a Christian to attend to the bride of Christ? In what ways are you preparing yourself and the church for his return?

3. How does your picture of eternity affect the life you want to live now? How can it change the way you think about joy?

CONCLUSION

"You make known to me the path of life; in your
presence there is fullness of joy; at your right hand
are pleasures forevermore." (Ps. 16:11, ESV)

God alone has a complete perspective on the path of life. We can tell stories, craft metaphors, and spend our lives as students of truth, but we'll never gain total access to the vantage point from which God observes life on the mountain.

Still, we can commit to learning. We can be intentional to pursue a deeper relationship with our Creator. We can listen to his leading. And as we do those things, God allows us to see bits and pieces of the bigger story, as told from his bird's-eye view. When we come to a deeper understanding of our place in God's story and position ourselves in the center of his presence, his word says that there we'll find fullness of joy.

"Fullness of joy" might sound an awful lot like a fountain, but I'm still not convinced that they are one and the same. Certainly, we know that "joy like a fountain" will happen in glory. But until then, I don't think it's necessary to assume that "fullness of joy" refers to a steady, vertical stream of giddiness that constantly bursts forth from the top of your head and cascades down your extremities to pool around your feet, or that anyone who gazes upon the spectacle of this magnificent human fountain will immediately experience the effects of your joy spilling over into their own life as well.

All things considered, I still think joy in this life is much more like a mountain. Because every step that we take on the mountain of life affords us an opportunity to choose joy, but that joy rarely comes easily. It's an uphill climb that, at times, requires an exorbitant amount of effort. In fact, so often in life, it feels as if the burden of choosing joy in the midst of suffering is heavier than the suffering itself.

And this is when we must be diligent to exercise joy as both a response *and* a responsibility. Rather than responding to our circumstances, it's our responsibility to cling to the truth of who God is and who he says we are so that we can find fullness of joy in his presence.

This fullness of joy is available to us in the midst of the trials and hardships of the mountain, but it doesn't happen overnight. It's a daily choice, an ongoing struggle, and an active surrender. But don't forget that when you engage with this process, to pursue the kind of biblical joy that we've discussed within the pages of this book, you'll grow in endurance, character, and hope.

Endurance gives us the guts and grit to push through the journey when life gets particularly difficult. It's a combination of courage and perseverance, working in us to propel us up the mountain against all odds.

Character develops as we follow the Guide and make use of his gear to navigate the challenges of this gruelling ascent. It empowers us to make wise decisions on the mountain that honor our fellow climbers as well as the King.

And hope? Well, hope is both the beginning and the end of this journey. Hope is what enables us to see the goal, the crown of life, and to "press on toward the... prize for which God has called [us] heavenward" (Phil. 3:14). Hope is found within the mysterious promise of our guaranteed victory over the dark secrets of the mountain. And hope climaxes in the assurance of the everlasting joy we'll experience in glory. Even though it may feel like a climb right now, we know that joy will be effortless in eternity.

For some of you, climbing through this book has been challenging enough on its own. If you're battling with mental illness right now, or even if you simply find yourself in a season of discouragement and despair, please know that I understand how painful the discussion of joy can be from that place. I'm profoundly moved by the fact that you've made it through this entire book. Thank you for allowing me into your journey.

Please know that I have been there. I've lived in that reality and come out the other side to find fullness of joy. Not joy that feels anything like a fountain, of course. This joy still feels daily like an uphill battle. But all the same, it is full, and rich, and beautiful because of the healing power of God at work in my life.

This kind of joy is possible for you too. And I'll be praying that you find it. I hope that this book has been a helpful tool in that journey for you, but I also urge you to seek professional help from a Christian counsellor who will eagerly assist you in your pursuit of biblical joy.

A REVOLUTION

When we began this journey, I spoke of a joy crisis that plagues our culture today. And though getting lost in the allegory of this book has, for me at least, provided a brief escape from the painful truth of this crisis, I know that it's time to step back to reality and fight for the revolution that this generation needs. Our world is rapidly drowning in an ocean of sorrows, and it seems as though the biblical narrative of joy is being swept under the rug when it should be cast out to sea as a life preserver to pull the victims of this crisis to safety.

That's our next move in advancing this revolution. We must radically implement the discipline of joy in our own lives so that we can reach out to the world around us with its message of hope and healing. For even more practical ideas on how to infuse your life with this kind of radical joy, I want to invite you to participate in my free 7-Day Joy Challenge, which you can find at: https://www.talasiguerra.com/7dayjoychallenge.

As Thomas Jefferson put it, "every generation needs a new revolution." And if joy really is so critical on the path of life, then joy is also a quintessential element of the revolution this generation needs.

So, let's get going! Let's fix our eyes on the goal and charge ahead in the liberating freedom of the guarantee. Let's keep in step with the Guide and employ the life-giving aid of the appropriate gear. Let's display all the guts and the grit that we've gained along this journey, and let's unleash the power of joy across the expanse of the mountain as we ascend into glory.

The joy revolution is now.

It's time to embrace joy like a mountain.

ACKNOWLEDGEMENTS

First and foremost, I'm grateful to God for revolutionizing my life with genuine, life-giving joy. What a deep honor and precious gift it has been to participate in his mission and to tell his story for his glory.

To my family, thank you. Ryan, my best friend and teammate in life, thank you for accompanying me on this unknown journey. Thank you for believing in me to pursue my calling, for making countless sacrifices to propel me forward, and for always pushing me to keep at it when I wanted to give up. Avra, thank you for being an endless source of joy in my life and for your grace and patience with me as I have poured myself into this project.

Mom and Dad, thank you for never giving up on me, despite the many reasons I have given you to do so. Your unconditional love and support have made it possible for me to pursue my dreams. To Pat and Patti Guerra, the best in-laws in the world, I couldn't have done this without your encouragement, help, and prayer.

Thanks to Laura, Bonnie, Charlotte, Anne, and Barry for offering insight and pushing me to improve the quality of my writing. Wayne, thank you for lending your tremendous editing skills to this project. Marcy, thank you for walking alongside me through this entire process and helping my dreams take flight. To the rest of the Self-Publishing School team, thank you for imparting your wisdom and knowledge to me so that I could do the same for others.

An enormous thank you to all of my amazing friends and family who provided childcare for Avra while I worked on this project. Your kindness will have ripple effects in eternity.

To the wonderful community of online readers who have supported me as a blogger and as a sharer of truth, thank you for your constant encouragement and affirmation. And to everyone who has ever read something that I have written and told me, "You should write a book one day," here it is. Thank you for believing in me and pushing me to get this book into your hands.

I am forever grateful.

ENDNOTES

CHAPTER 1: THE GENESIS

1 Murphy, Carrie. "This Is How Joy Affects Your Body." *Healthline*, 27 June 2018, www.healthline.com/health/affects-of-joy#1.

2 Coyle, Daisy. "How Being Happy Makes You Healthier." *Healthline*, Healthline Media, 27 Aug. 2017, www.healthline.com/nutrition/happiness-and-health#section3.

3 Hoomans, Joel. "35,000 Decisions: The Great Choices of Strategic Leaders." *Leading Edge Journal*, 20 Mar. 2015, go.roberts.edu/leadingedge/the-great-choices-of-strategic-leaders.

4 To learn more about Orange Kids, access www.ThinkOrange.com

5 "Mental Disorders Affect One in Four People." *World Health Organization*, World Health Organization, 29 July 2013, www.who.int/whr/2001/media_centre/press_release/en/.

6 "Mental Health by the Numbers." *NAMI*, National Alliance on Mental Health, Sept. 2019, www.nami.org/Learn-More/Mental-Health-By-the-Numbers.

7 "Fast Facts about Mental Illness." *CMHA National*, Canadian Mental Health Association, cmha.ca/fast-facts-about-mental-illness.

8 "Study of Acute Mental Illness and Christian Faith." *Lifeway Research*, Lifeway Research/Focus on the Family, lifewayresearch.com/wp-content/uploads/2014/09/Acute-Mental-Illness-and-Christian-Faith-Research-Report-1.pdf.

CHAPTER 2: THE GOAL

9   History.com Editors. "Henry VIII." *HISTORY*, A&E Television Networks, 9 Nov. 2009, www.history.com/topics/british-history/henry-viii.

10   Musker, John and Ron Clements, directors. *Aladdin*. Walt Disney Pictures, 1992.

11   "Lessons from the Ledge: Alison Levine at TEDxMidwest." YouTube, uploaded by TEDx Talks, 26 June 2012, www.youtube.com/watch?v=6hUybmqUVmM&t=737s.

CHAPTER 3: THE GUARANTEE

12   "Japan WW2 Soldier Who Refused to Surrender Hiroo Onoda Dies." *BBC News*, 17 Jan. 2014, www.bbc.com/news/world-asia-25772192.

CHAPTER 4: THE GUIDE

13   Woodward, Aylin. "What Happens to Your Body in Mount Everest's 'Death Zone,' Where 11 People Have Died in the Past Week." *Business Insider*, 28 May 2019, www.businessinsider.com/mount-everest-death-zone-what-happens-to-body-2019-5.

14   Lee, Nathaniel, and Jessica Orwig. "The World's Tallest Mountains like Mount Everest and K2 Have a 'Death Zone' - Here's a First-Hand Account of What It's Like." *Business Insider*, 29 May 2019, www.businessinsider.com/mount-everest-death-zone-first-hand-account-2017-9.

15   Daumal, René, and Roger Shattuck. "Notes." In *Mount Analogue: An Authentic Narrative*, Stuart, 1959, p. 103.

16   "Unsung Heroes: The Sherpas of Everest." *Populous*, Populous, 23 Oct. 2019, populous.com/unsung-heroes-the-sherpas-of-everest.

CHAPTER 5: THE GEAR

17   Nag, Oishimaya Sen. "What Is an Icefall?" *WorldAtlas*, WorldAtlas, 9
     June 2017, www.worldatlas.com/articles/what-is-an-icefall.html.

18   Dixit, Kunda. "In Mount Everest Region, World's Highest Glaciers
     Are Melting." *InsideClimate News*, Nepali Times, 20 June 2019, inside
     climatenews.org/news/26112018/mount-everest-photos-world-highest-
     glacier-climate-change-khombu-icefall-climbing-route.

19   National Geographic Society. "Kilimanjaro." *National Geographic
     Society*, 6 Sept. 2019, www.nationalgeographic.org/encyclopedia/
     kilimanjaro/.

20   "How Long Does It Take to Climb Kilimanjaro?" *Ultimate Kilimanjaro®-
     The #1 Guide Service on Mount Kilimanjaro*, Ultimate Kilimanjaro,
     www.ultimatekilimanjaro.com/days.htm.

21   Heiting, Gary. "Snow Blindness: How to Prevent Sunburned Eyes."
     All About Vision, AAV Media, LLC., Aug. 2017, www.allaboutvision.
     com/conditions/snowblind.htm.

CHAPTER 6: THE GUTS

22   Lewis, C.S. "Dark Island." In *The Voyage of the Dawn Treader,* Scholastic
     Inc., 1995, pp. 176-189

CHAPTER 7: THE GRIT

23   Duckworth, Angela. "What Is Grit?" *Angela Duckworth*, 2020,
     angeladuckworth.com/qa/#faq-125.

24   Acuff, Jon. "Mastering." In *Start*, edited by Brent Cole and Darcie
     Clemen, Ramsey Press, The Lampo

25   Group, 2013, p. 135.

26   Barnes, Albert. "James Chapter 1." *Sacred Texts*, www.sacred-texts.
     com/bib/cmt/barnes/jam001.htm.

CHAPTER 8: THE GLORY

27 Piper, John. "What Is God's Glory?" *Desiring God*, 22 July 2014, www. desiringgod.org/interviews/what-is-gods-glory--2.

28 *Life Application Study Bible: New International Version.* Tyndale House Publishers, 2017, p. 1587.

WORK WITH TALASI

Talasi lives to communicate life-changing truth in relevant ways that inspire, challenge, and awaken others to live out their God-given purpose. She would love to partner with you at your next conference, retreat, or other event. For speaking inquiries, please visit Talasi's website at: https://www.talasiguerra.com/booking

CONNECT ONLINE

Instagram: @talasiguerra
Website: www.talasiguerra.com

CAN YOU HELP?

Thank You for Reading *Joy Like a Mountain.*

I love hearing what my readers have to say, and I would be deeply grateful for your feedback!

I need your input to make the next version of this book and my future books better.

Please leave me an honest review on Amazon letting me know what you thought of the book.

Thank you so much for reading and for joining the joy revolution!

—Talasi Guerra